KILKENNY

No. 3

1 JERSEY,
14 MEN,
34 ALL-IRELAND TITLES

DERMOT KAVANAGH

IRISH SPORTS PUBLISHING

Published by Irish Sports Publishing (ISP)
Unit 11, Tandy's Lane
Lucan, Co Dublin
Ireland
www.irishsportspublishing.com

First published, 2012

While every effort has been made to contact and acknowledge copyright holders of third party materials included in the book, it has proven difficult to track down a small minority. Please contact Irish Sports Publishing if you believe the book includes material of yours that has not been acknowledged, and every effort will be made to correct this in future reprints.

A CIP record for this book is available from the British Library

ISBN 978-0-9573954-0-4

Printed in Ireland with Print Procedure Ltd
Typesetting Jessica Maile
Cover Anu Design www.anu-design.ie
Photographs: Inpho Sports Agency and Dermot Kavanagh's own collection.

DEDICATION

Not for fame or fortune,
Not for place or rank,
Not lured by ambition,
Or goaded by necessity,
But in simple obedience to Duty
As they understood it
These men suffered all,
Sacrificed all,
Dared all.

This dedication, etched on the Memorial to the Dead of the Confederate States Army at Arlington Cemetery, Washington, is humbly appropriated to honour the personal and sporting lives of the 14 players who are the subject matter of this study.

ACKNOWLEDGMENTS

Sincere thanks is extended to the following who, by their own individual contributions, helped enormously to bring this publication to completion: Marie Butler; Sean and Mary Holohan; Peter O'Reilly; Fan Larkin; Gerry Hennessy; Martin Hayden; Tom Walsh; Pa Dillon; Paddy Butler; Paddy Buggy; Babs Whelan; Mary and Nicky Orr; Paddy Prendergast; Brian Cody; Pat Dwyer; Noel Hickey; JJ Delany; Gerry O'Neill; Billy Norris; Jim Fogarty; Kilkenny Library personnel Jean Croughan, Damien Brett and Alicia Dunphy; Patrick O'Sullivan; Honor Martin; Traolach Martin; Tom Fleming; PJ Garvan; Weeshie Fogarty (Radio Kerry); John Lenihane (Fitzgerald Stadium, Killarney), and the staff of Rothe House, Kilkenny.

—⚏—

SPONSORS

I am extremely grateful to the following whose financial contributions helped considerably to defray some of the expenses incurred in the writing of this book:

Jim Morrissey, Building Contractor, Tramore
Messers Tierney O'Neill, Builders Contractors, Inistioge
Clara GAA Club
Carrickshock United GAA Club
Dunamaggin GAA Club
James Stephens GAA Club
The Rower/Inistioge GAA Club
Kilkenny GAA County Board

CONTENTS

INTRODUCTION

"A people without a territory is like a man without a shadow."
Leon Pinsker

Leon Pinsker, a Zionist sympathiser, wrote the above words in 1881. Pinsker was an avid supporter of a permanent homeland for the Jewish people who, he said, "simply wanted a place to belong to".

The 14 players profiled in this study had no difficulties in identifying the territory each of them belonged to, or which territory they each had to defend. To them, territory had many meanings. It was a home, a townland, a parish, a county, and a country. All clearly identifiable! In a sporting sense, territory had, for them, another meaning – it related to a rectangular area of ground measuring 75 square yards fronting the goalposts at either end of a hurling pitch. Thankfully, from Kilkenny's standpoint, when charged to do so, all 14 players were prepared to stretch every sinew, flex every muscle, and shed tears and blood if necessary in order to defend that rectangle

To each of those 14 players that rectangular area of ground was sacred. Each of them was instinctively aware that failure to successfully defend it was not an option. Even in the face of inevitable defeat, which confronted each man from time to time, each of them strove to ensure that whatever section of the field was to be surrendered, theirs would be the last... if ever!

From Jack Rochford's time to that of Noel Hickey, 34 senior All-Ireland titles have been won. In each of those wins every one of the 14 full-backs featured were the best men then available for selection. Better men were not ignored. That none of the 14 chosen was replaced in any of those wins, through lack of ability, form, or effort, is a lasting tribute to each and every one of them.

There is no specific template for a Kilkenny All-Ireland winning full-back. They can come in all shapes and sizes. Witness the lithe, sinewy Jack

Rochford, the 5' 7" Paddy Larkin, the 6' 2" Pa Dillon, the burly Jim 'Link' Walsh, the tall and languid Brian Cody, the granite like 5' 10" Noel Hickey, or the fleet-footed JJ Delaney. Neither did they all originate from similar backgrounds. However, with six farmers in the group perhaps that is what Dr Croke had in mind when he said, in a roundabout way, that the major flaw in Irishmen playing 'foreign games' was that those games were 'not racy of the soil'. Apart from those six farmers, that the remainder of this elite group contained a tailor, a baker, a plasterer, a driver, a teacher, an industrial employee, a road surface contractor, and a college graduate clearly testifies to the eclectic composition of hurling's workforce.

In the relative comfort that the majority of us now enjoy, one must marvel at the commitment and single-mindedness of the original members of the elite group. Players such as Jack Rochford, John Holohan, Peter O'Reilly, Paddy Larkin and 'Diamond' Hayden devoted themselves to hurling at times when merely making a living to support themselves and their families was a struggle, given the unforgiving economic conditions of their times. Modern-day players who whine over the sacrifices they imagine they pay to play elite sports of whatever disciplines, would do well to respect the times in which they live their sporting lives.

Of Kilkenny's 36 parishes, Johnstown leads the way with three of the elite group – John Holohan, Nicky Orr and JJ Delaney all hail from that northern hamlet. Curiously, a mere eight other parishes supplied players to those victorious teams.

Every journey, whether long or short, begins with a single step. Who can tell where the journey that Jack Rochford began at Deerpark, Carrick-on-Suir, on Sunday, June 24, 1906 (the date of the 1904 All-Ireland hurling final) will end? That is the only unknown. What is known is that the journey to date has been exhilarating to read about, to witness part of it, and to celebrate all of it.

To those remarkable 14 players and their comrades, buiochas uile daoibh

Dermot Kavanagh

PROLOGUE

"Hurling is one of the greatest games on earth. Its simplicity, the strength and swiftness of its players, their apparent angelic impetuosity, their apparent recklessness of life and limb, their magic skill, their wondrous dexterity of hand and marvellous accuracy of eye produce a thrilling, spectacular effect, and place the game in the front rank of outstanding sports.

The game has been more closely associated with patriotic service to Ireland's cause than any other pastime. That was not only because hurling men were physically fit and blessed with a heroic spirit, but because it was in Ireland's heroic age that hurling was born."

From the bi-lingual Australian Newspaper, *An Dorn Feinne* (1924)

—⚬—

Hurling is our game, the game of the Irish people. This spectacular, free-flowing, skilful game played on lush green fields captures and embodies what it means to be Irish. It connects family to townlands, townlands to parish, and parish to a county in a matchless and beguiling manner

Hurling is part of us.

We love playing it.

We love watching it.

We love reading and talking about it.

It is such a part of us that historians and anthropologists have, over the years, tried to capture its essence, its meaning.

Hurling affects us in many ways.

It thrills us.

It enlivens us.

It fills us with anticipation, fear, joy, heartbreak and exultation, in no particular order, and usually all in the course of a single game. Songwriters and musicians have, from the game's earliest days, extolled us with the feats of the great players, together with lyrical narratives of memorable wins and shattering defeats.

We love hurling because it is real and has substance. This love has been handed down through the generations. We are forever hitting a ball with our hurley, either on our own, or with siblings or friends. We win. We lose. We are happy. We are sad. But hurling, the game and its traditions, gives us more than visual stimulation and emotion. It appeals to something within us.

As it is difficult to adequately explain the essence of the game, perhaps the best approach is to attend a game, or to follow a parish team for a year, or to spend a lifetime immersed in hurling. The game has soul.

To witness an Under-10 training session is an exhilarating experience. The trainer, usually a former player, saddened that he can no longer play the game, is nonetheless excited at the prospect that the boys and girls under his care will love hurling as he does. Hoping that they will feel that the game has something for them, as it has for him. The kids' joy is his joy. Those kids, who have probably slept with their hurleys, the rest of their gear having been neatly laid out beside the freshly polished boots before going to bed.

Hurling is a game in which people of different shapes can find a place. Yet each player must strive to master the many skills required – athleticism, strength with subtlety, fitness, coordination between hand and eye, an ability to gain possession of the ball while it's in the air, or on the ground, even if it's travelling at over 100 mph. All of this, despite being closely marked! The two skills of the game, which distinguishes the piano player from the piano pusher is, initially, the first touch to control and collect the ball, and, secondly, the accuracy of the strike off either hand. The prototype of the former is Henry Shefflin, while the rest of the hurling fraternity to a large degree comprise the latter.

The hurler must also possess a mysterious gift. He must be able to read the play. He, and he alone, must decide when and where to move. He must decide whether to stand back or enter the fray. He must decide instantly whether to strike long for a score or for territory, or short to a better-placed colleague. He must see the players ahead of him, who themselves are reading his play. Then he must perform the skill. All so quickly. All so accurately. All so adeptly. All while being under pressure from harrying opponents.

In hurling strongholds, the hurling club remains the lifeblood of the community. Specks on the map that have lost their post offices, local shops, petrol stations and, sometimes, even their schools and pubs, have somehow managed to retain their hurling clubs. These clubs aren't just about hitting a ball or winning a championship. They represent the very core of life in that area, pulling together to survive in hard times and to prosper when life's chips fall in their favour.

It is unequivocally accepted that hurling played an important part in the life of pre-Christian Ireland. For example, provisions were made in The Brehon Laws for compensation for injuries sustained in hurling matches. The Battle of Moytura, circa 2000BC, was, as legend holds, preceded by a hurling match. The Statutes of Kilkenny, 1136, outlawed hurling on the grounds that, "too much hurling led to a neglect of military service". In the 14th century, Catholics in Armagh were threatened with excommunication if they played hurling as the Church feared that participation in hurling would lead to, "violence, insobriety and possibly extreme nationalistic activities".

With hurling's centuries old lineage, the formal establishment of Australian Rules (1859), Association Football (1863), Rugby Football (1871), and the GAA (1884) itself, appear as mere modern creations.

Wars, famine, state and church intervention, recessions, emigration, occasional bouts of GAA administrative myopia, social, educational and sporting snobbery, the Celtic Tiger, FIFA and IRB World Cups, and numerous other influences have, over the years, all challenged the very existence of hurling. None has succeeded.

Hurling is more than a game. It is of Ireland. It is of Kilkenny, and of every parish within it. To paraphrase Jack Rochford, legendary Kilkenny full-back of the 1904-1913 era, on his county's proficiency at hurling: "We cannot help it. We are born hurlers, inheritors of a proud tradition, one that we will never betray."

Dermot Kavanagh

PART ONE

Those Who Have Passed

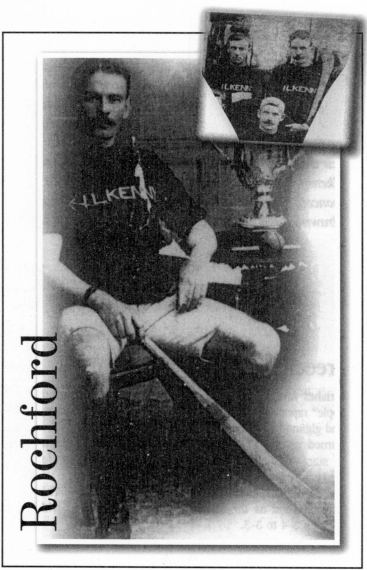

Rochford

Jack Rochford, who played with Threecastles, Erin's Own and Tullaroan in his career, was the lynchpin of a Kilkenny defence that became almost impregnable, as the winning of seven All-Ireland titles between 1904 and 1913 testifies. insert photograph: Jack is pictured with Dick 'Drooge' Walsh (left) and Sim Walton (front).

chapter 1

JACK ROCHFORD
1904, 1905, 1907, 1909, 1911, 1912 and 1913

The arrival of Jack Rochford on the inter-county scene in 1902 and the subsequent creation of Kilkenny's first 'Golden Era' soon afterwards are closely linked events. In the previous decade, prior to Jack's accession to the team, Kilkenny had lost four All-Ireland finals and one 'Home' final, all by considerable margins. In time Jack became the lynchpin of a defence that became almost impregnable as the winning of seven All-Ireland titles between 1904 and 1913 testifies. With the advent of Jack, and such players as Sim Walton, Paddy 'Icy' Lannigan, the Doyle brothers, Dan Stapelton, Jack Anthony, Jimmy 'the Wren' Kelly, and others, Kilkenny were transformed from serial losers to consistent winners. Those title wins in 1904, 1905, 1907, 1909, 1911, 1912 and 1913 also transformed Kilkenny from a county with a hitherto impressive Gaelic Football pedigree, to an almost exclusive hurling one.

It is arguable that, were it not for some avoidable outbursts of petulance and selfishness by some of the major forces within Kilkenny hurling during that 1904-1913 era, additional All-Ireland titles would have come the county's way.

In 1906 the Tullaroan players withdrew from the team prior to the Leinster final against Dublin in protest over team selection policy. Two years later the County Board withdrew the team from the Leinster final in response to the Leinster Council's ruling that Kilkenny were not entitled to claim custody of the unique Railway Shield, despite having supplied 15 of the 17 players who had won the trophy outright for Leinster earlier that year. The Council later reversed that decision.

In 1910 the influential Doyle brothers, from Mooncoin, withdrew from the team to play the Leinster semi-final, in protest over the County Board's arrangements for the pending county final. And, finally, Sim Walton, Dick Dowling and Jack were inexplicably absent for the 1914 Leinster final team. Significantly, Kilkenny failed to win even a Leinster title in each year where unrest existed. Clearly, with more diplomacy and unity of purpose, and less politics, even greater heights of sporting achievement could, and should, have been scaled.

Jack commenced his adult hurling career in 1901, retiring in 1916. He became the leading full-back of his era and, despite almost a century having elapsed since his retirement, and over 50 years since his death, he is still acknowledged as one of the most celebrated full-backs the game has known. His harvest of seven All-Ireland medals was a record he shared with three of his Kilkenny team-mates, Sim Walton, Dick 'Drooge' Walsh and Dick Doyle, a record that was not equalled until 1953 by Christy Ring.

—⁓—

During my research into this project I had the honour and privilege of meeting Jack's youngest daughter, Marie Butler, who resides in the leafy Dublin suburb of Clontarf. Marie holds treasured memories of time spent with her father and is fully aware of, and justifiably proud of, his hurling achievements.

Jack was born in Tulla, Threecastles, on April 24,1882. His father, Michael,

was a master journeyman tailor, who travelled widely in the course of his work. Jack's mother, Catherine, formerly White, originally from Ballyouskill, was a cousin of Martin White (subsequently a Kilkenny hurling hero of the 1930s). In addition to Jack, the Rochfords had two other children, Kathleen and Bridget.

Jack attended two primary schools in the area, Clinstown and Ballydaniel.

Immediately on leaving school he began his working life, following in his father's footsteps.

During Jack's teenage years the formal administration of underage sport was practically non-existent, especially in rural areas such as Tulla. It was, therefore, incumbent on any rural-based boy or girl who aspired to follow a sporting discipline of whatever type to make their own arrangements as to practise and training with siblings, friends and neighbours. Jack's two sporting passions, hurling and cricket, games then operating on almost an equal footing in his north Kilkenny parish, were pursued and practised in adjoining fields and farmyards. In time Jack's potential as a hurler was noted and, in his late teenage years, he played some games for Tullaroan, a neighbouring club. However, when a club was formed in his native parish he immediately enlisted. His association with Threecastles had begun.

Jack's first major hurling adventure ended in disappointment when Threecastles were defeated by Tullaroan in the 1901 county senior final. His outstanding displays in that campaign earned him selection on the county team for the 1902 Championship. That adventure also ended in disappointment, when Kilkenny lost the Leinster final to Dublin. The following year Jack won his first provincial medal but, shortly after achieving that milestone, he endured the ignominy of Kilkenny's obliteration by Cork in the All-Ireland 'Home' final, on a scoreline of 8-9 to 0-8.

If Jack and his colleagues then felt that following that defeat, and those of the previous decade, they and Kilkenny were never destined to make the breakthrough, it would have been quite understandable. Four All-Ireland final defeats and the recent mauling by Cork made for depressing reading. However, little did he and his comrades realise how quickly their fortunes would change, and that, of the following 11 Championships, Kilkenny would win seven. By the conclusion of that successful run in 1913, Kilkenny had overtaken Cork and lay one title behind Tipperary in the Roll of Honour. Sadly, and as noted, the success strike rate could, and should, have been greater.

Kilkenny's 1911 title arrived courtesy of a Central Council decision. Who is to say that, considering the team's recently acquired record in finals, they would not have won it on the field had their All-Ireland final opponents,

Limerick, not refused to play the rescheduled game?

Kilkenny achieved their first three-in-a-row in November 1913, only the second county to do so. However, their circuitous route to that honour is worth recording. At the Annual Congress held in Dublin's City Hall on March 13, it was decided to allow one team each from Scotland and England to participate in that year's Championship. Jack and his comrades had, therefore, to undertake the following journey en route to retaining their successive titles:

1. June 15 – defeated Glasgow in Glasgow, 10-6 to 5-7
2. July 13 – defeated Laois in Portlaoise, 8-3 to 2-6
3. August 4 – defeated Lancashire in Liverpool, 4-4 to 0-3
4. August 24 – drew with Dublin in Leinster final at Wexford, 1-0 to 0-3
5. September 28 – defeated Dublin in replay at Wexford, 7-5 to 2-1
6. November 2 – defeated Tipperary in All-Ireland final at Croke Memorial Park, 2-4 to 1-2.

Curiously, there was some element of confusion amongst certain sections of the media and the public as regards the actual status of the games against Glasgow and Lancashire. In a clear attempt to ensure that the players were properly focused on the challenge facing them in Glasgow, *The Kilkenny People* issued the following warning: "A good deal depends on this match. Few people are aware that, if Kilkenny are beaten, that they are out of the Championship."

Later in the year, the same paper reviewed the Lancashire game as an All-Ireland semi-final, despite the Leinster final not having yet being played. Other innovations introduced at that 1913 Congress saw the introduction of the 15-a-side teams, the re-naming of Jones' Road as 'The Croke Memorial Park', and, following a successful Cork motion, it became mandatory for counties to adopt and register distinctive county colours.

For the 1913 final, the County Board allotted a sum or IR£60 to enable the players to undertake two weeks of 'collective' training to prepare for the game. The Tullaroan, Threecastles and Erin's Own players were based in the city, training in St James' Park, while the southern based players trained in

Mooncoin. Following Kilkenny's record-equalling 1913 win, *The Kilkenny People* produced an outstandingly lyrical match report under the heading 'The Fall of Toom' (Tipperary were represented by Toomevara). In relation to Jack the writer noted: "Jack, the sole representative of the hamlet of Threecastles, was at his zenith on Sunday. When all the backs were beaten, Rochford was always in the gap, and, when it came to sprinting, was equal, if not faster, than his opponent. It was good to see him playing his tricks in the concluding stages."

Tipperary were strongly fancied to win that 1913 final, following their heavy defeat of Cork in the Munster final. Free scoring full-forward, Bud O'Dwyer, was expected to lead the famous 'Greyhounds' to victory. Such was Jack's domination of O'Dwyer over the hour that, when he was leaving the field following the game, O'Dwyer was reported by *The Kilkenny People* as remarking: "Before this game I thought I was the best full-forward around, but now I doubt if I will get my place on the team."

In tandem with his inter-county career, Jack was equally successful at inter-provincial level. In 1905, an inter-provincial Championship was inaugurated for which the impressive and unique Railway Shield was donated by The Great Southern and Western Rail Company. The rules of the competition stated that the first province to win it twice in succession, or three times in all, would retain permanent custody of the Shield. Leinster won out in 1905 and 1907, with Munster winning in 1906 and 1908. It was then decided that, following Munster's second win, they and Leinster would meet later that year to decide the Shield's outright winners. Thus, on June 21, at St James' Park, Kilkenny, before an attendance of over 15,000, Leinster won an enthralling game by 0-14 to Munster 2-5, with Jack imperious at full-back. In a somewhat partisan report, *The Kilkenny People* described the game as "the greatest match on record, played amidst unparalleled scenes of enthusiasm". At the competition's conclusion Jack had added three prestigious inter-provincial medals to his collection.

At club level Jack experienced mixed results. He played county Championship hurling with three separate clubs – Threecastles, Erin's Own and Tullaroan. In total, Jack played in five county finals, winning with Threecastles in 1903 and Tullaroan in 1915, while losing in 1901 and 1908 with Threecastles, and, in 1914, with Erin's Own.

That Jack was his own man – both on and off the field – and one not to be second-guessed, was well established. In addition to withdrawing from the 1914 Leinster final, he also withdrew from the team shortly before the 1916 All-Ireland final, apparently following a dispute with his long-term friend, Sim Walton, over team selection. Sadly, but somewhat predictably given the single-mindedness of both men, they never subsequently reconciled their differences. However, their paths did cross again, but in rather poignant circumstances. Following Jack's death in 1953, Sim requested permission from Catherine Rochford if he could act as pallbearer at her husband's funeral. Catherine was only too happy to oblige.

Following his retirement from the game in 1916, Jack pursued his profession with the same zeal which hallmarked his hurling. His travels took him to Dublin where he met, and subsequently married, Catherine Gallagher, a teacher from Glenties, Co Donegal. Four of Jack and Catherine's five children, Michael, Kitty, Christina and Carmel were born in Dublin. When the family moved to Kilkenny city in the late 1920s their youngest daughter, Marie, was born. The family's first home in the city was in High Street, a property which Jack leased from his 1905 winning captain, Dan Stapelton.

The Rochford family later moved back to the old family home at Tulla. That property was subsequently sold, the family moving back to the city, purchasing a house at No. 9, Lord Edward Street, where Jack and Catherine lived out their lives

Following her marriage, Catherine had to retire from teaching in compliance with the Department of Education's draconian regulations relating to married women remaining in the public sector workforce. Jack thus became the family's sole earner, working mainly from home. One of his more financially rewarding commissions was tending to the cassocks and uniforms of the large numbers of students then attending the diocesan seminary at St Kieran's College. Marie recently wistfully remarked that "such a commission would not be worth much nowadays".

When Jack's playing days were over he developed a keen interest in the physical fitness aspect of the game. He was co-trainer of the 1922 All-Ireland winning team, a role he also played with the 1931 team. In the early 1940s

The Kilkenny People ran a series of monthly articles, entitled 'The Gaels of the Black and Amber', written by Gus Murray. Jack was the source of most of the material used in relation to the 1904-1913 era. Marie recalls that her father's assistance with those articles cost him the friendship of the prominent Kennealy family, the proprietors of Kilkenny's other weekly newspaper, *The Kilkenny Journal*.

Jack retained a sharp interest in hurling throughout his life. Marie recalls travelling to all the major games with him and fondly remembers great evenings in the company of such greats as 'Drooge' Walsh, the Doyles, John T. Power, Lory Meagher, Mick Mackey, 'Diamond' Hayden, and many other household names. In the late 1940s and early 1950s, Marie also remembers the three Rackard brothers as being very frequent and very welcome visitors to the Rochford household whenever they were in the locality, either on business or for matches.

—∿—

Marie also remembers her father as being a multi-talented, fun-loving, independent-minded man of his time. In addition to his tailoring and hurling exploits, Marie recalls her father as an accomplished concertina player, as well as being a keen golfer and cricketer. During Jack's playing days the majority of hurlers openly played cricket, despite the GAA's 'foreign games' ban. Such was the popularity of cricket in the area, and the positive social interaction between the various strands of society which those games generated, that the County Board largely turned a blind eye to the frequent breaches of its rules, particularly when prominent hurlers were concerned.

There was a mischievous side to Jack's personality, one that was best countered in similar fashion. In February, 1913, he wrote to the County Secretary intimating his desire to "resign" from the county team. Amongst the reasons quoted for his proposed "resignation" Jack wrote: "I cannot see what I want in keeping young lads off the pitch when I am satisfied with the time I was on it."

When Jack's letter was later read out at the next County Board meeting it elicited the following exchange:

Chairman: "I don't think it will be possible to keep Jack down."

Mr Lalor, Threecastles: "I would not accept his resignation."

Chairman: "We will treat it as a joke."

The meeting unanimously decided to reject Jack's proposed "resignation".

Though of a lithe, sinewy build, Jack revelled in the rough and tumble action that then characterised the goalmouth exchanges. He had incredibly quick hands that enabled him to almost effortlessly dispossess his opponent before executing his legendary clearances. He became a leader of a generation of Kilkenny hurlers who broke the county's losing mentality, and sowed the seeds of a winning approach, one that has endured for over 100 years, down to the present days of Henry Shefflin and comrades.

Jack died on October 17, 1953, after a short illness. He was buried in Tulla graveyard beside his parents, Michael and Catherine. His widow, Catherine, who died in 1982 in her 100th year, also rests there.

Two incidents surrounding her father's funeral were, recalls Marie, especially pleasing to the family. One was the number of hurlers, both young and old, and from all the game's strongholds, who attended, paying tribute, as it were, "to a fallen colleague". Secondly, the number of business houses in the city that closed their stores on the day of the funeral to enable staff and customers to pay their respects.

Sadly, only one of Jack's many medals is still held by the family. Over time Jack gave the rest away, usually to visitors from abroad, particularly visiting priests who were regular callers to the Rochford household.

Sports people, irrespective of their own achievements and awards, will invariably acknowledge that the plaudits they cherish most are those they receive from their peers. Thus it is worth noting the following tribute Jack received from his 1905 winning captain, Dan Stapelton, as appeared in *The Gaelic Echo* in August 1940: "Jack Rochford was the most brilliant full back of his era. When all seemed lost Jack had the most unusual habit of nipping in with his hurley to turn the ball only a matter of inches, causing his opponent to miss. I often watched Jack juggle with the ball to the bewilderment of his opponents. I played in front of Jack and tried to carry out my instructions which were, simply, to protect Jack at all costs."

Perhaps it is advisable to leave the final words to Jack himself. In the summer of 1937 a builders' strike in Dublin delayed the completion of the new Cusack Stand in Croke Park, causing the All-Ireland hurling final between Kilkenny and Tipperary to be switched to Fitzgerald Stadium, Killarney. In its extensive and impressive pre-match coverage, *The Kerryman* reproduced an article written by Jack some years previously, under the heading: 'Jack Rochford Tells Kilkenny's Secrets'.

In the article Jack states: "There are no secrets to Kilkenny hurling. We practise night, noon and morning. The local Championships have fitted us well for inter-county hurling. We revel in the daring and manly deeds of the hurling field. We are born hurlers. We cannot help it. We are the inheritors of a proud tradition, one which we will never betray."

In essence, Jack Rochford was paying tribute to every Kilkenny person who ever wielded the hurley, irrespective of the grade, or whether competitively, or merely for pleasure.

CAREER HIGHLIGHTS

All-Ireland senior winner: 1904, 1905, 1907, 1909, 1911, 1912 and 1913

All-Ireland 'Home' finalist: 1903

Leinster Championship winner: 1903, 1904, 1905, 1907, 1909, 1911, 1912, 1913 and 1916.

County senior finalist: Threecastles – 1901, 1903 and 1908; Erin's Own – 1909; Tullaroan – 1915

County Senior Final Wins: 1903, 1915.

Railway Shield winner: 1905, 1907 and 1908

All-Ireland final co-trainer: 1922, 1931

ALL-IRELAND WINNING TEAMS

1904

June 24, 1906

Kilkenny 1-9 Cork 1-8

Deerpark, Carrick on Suir

Attendance 8,000 (est.)

Kilkenny: Pat 'Fox' Maher (Tullaroan), Jack Hoyne (Tullaroan), Jack Rochford (Threecastles), Paddy 'Icy' Lannigan (Erin's Own), Dan Grace (Tullaroan), Dick 'Drooge' Walsh (Mooncoin), Eddie Doyle (Mooncoin), Pat Fielding (Mooncoin), Jim Lalor (Threecastles), Pat Saunders (Tullaroan), Dan Stapelton (Erin's Own), Martin Lalor (Threecastles), Sim Walton (Tullaroan), Jack Anthony (Piltown), Ger Doheny (Tullaroan), Dick Brennan (Erin's Own), Dick Doyle (Mooncoin) .

Subs: John James Brennan (Erin's Own), Pat Clohosey (Tullaroan), Jim Dunne (Tullaroan) replaced Stapelton (injured 60 mins.)

1905

April 17, 1907

Cork 5-10 Kilkenny 3-13

Tipperary Town

Attendance 5,500 (est.)

Kilkenny: Dick 'Drooge' Walsh (Mooncoin), Jack Hoyne (Tullaroan), Jack Rochford (Threecastles), Paddy 'Icy' Lannigan (Erin's Own), Dan Kennedy (Erin's Own), Eddie Doyle (Mooncoin), Tom Kenny (Erin's Own), Matt Gargan (Erin's Own), Joe Glennon (Threecastles), Jim Lalor (Threecastles), Dan Stapelton, captain (Erin's Own), Martin Lalor (Threecastles), Sim Walton (Tullaroan), Jack Anthony (Piltown), John James Brennan (Erin's Own), Jimmy 'The Wren' Kelly (Mooncoin), Dick Doyle (Mooncion).

Kilkenny lodged an objection on the grounds that Cork panellist, Daniel McCarthy was illegal due to British Army connections. Cork counter-objected on the question of Matt Gargan's legality. The Central Council upheld both objections and ordered a replay.

1905 All-Ireland final replay
June 30, 1907
Kilkenny 7-7 Cork 2- 9
Fraher Field, Dungarvan
Attendance 10,000 (est.)

Kilkenny: Ned Teehan (Tullaroan), Jack Hoyne (Tullaroan), Jack Rochford (Threecastles), Paddy 'Icy' Lannigan (Erin's Own), Dan Grace (Tullaroan), Dick 'Drooge' Walsh (Mooncoin), Eddie Doyle (Mooncoin), Dan Kennedy (Erin's Own), Tom Kenny (Erin's Own), Jim Lalor (Threecastles), Dan Stapelton, captain (Erin's Own), Martin Lalor (Threecastles), Sim Walton (Tullaroan), Jack Anthony (Piltown), John James Brennan (Erin's Own), Jimmy 'The Wren' Kelly (Mooncoin), Dick Doyle (Mooncoin).

Subs: Willie Culleton (Erin's Own), Jack Keoghan (Tullaroan), Tom Murphy (Threecastles) replaced Stapelton (injured 7 mins).

1907
June 21, 1908
Kilkenny 3-12 Cork 4-8
Fraher Field, Dungarvan
Attendance 15,000 (est.)

Kilkenny: John T Power (Piltown), Jack Keoghan (Tullaroan), Jack Rochford (Threecastles), Paddy 'Icy' Lannigan (Erin's Own), Dan Grace (Tullaroan), Dick 'Drooge' Walsh, captain (Mooncoin), Eddie Doyle (Mooncoin), Dick Doherty (Mooncoin), Matt Gargan (Erin's Own), Dan Kennedy (Erin's Own, Dan Stapelton (Erin's Own), Tom Kenny (Erin's Own), Sim Walton (Tullaroan), Jack Anthony (Piltown), Mick Doyle (Mooncoin), Jimmy 'The Wren' Kelly (Mooncoin), Dick Doyle (Mooncoin).

Subs: Dick Brennan (Erin's Own), Jack Hoyne (Tullaroan), Jim Lalor (Threecastles).

1909

December 12

Kilkenny 4-6 Tipperary 0-12

Cork Athletic Grounds

Attendance 'enormous', as per match report

Kilkenny: Jim Dunphy (Mooncoin), Jack Keoghan (Tullaroan), Jack Rochford (Threecastles), Paddy 'Icy' Lannigan (Erin's Own), Dan Kennedy (Tullaroan), Dick 'Drooge' Walsh, captain (Mooncoin), Eddie Doyle (Mooncoin), Joe Delahunty (Mooncoin), Dick Doherty (Mooncoin), Matt Gargan (Erin's Own), Jim Ryan (Mooncoin), Mick Shortall (Erin's Own), Sim Walton (Tullaroan), Dick Doyle (Mooncoin), Bill Hennebry (Mooncoin), Jimmy 'The Wren' Kelly (Mooncoin), Mick Doyle (Mooncoin). Subs: Dick Grace (Tullaroan), replaced Doherty (injured half time), Tom McCormack (Erin's Own).

Unavailable: John T Power, Jack Anthony and Jack Butler (all Piltown) whose club refused them permission to play following a controversial county semi-final game against Mooncoin. Tom Kenny (Erin's Own) cried off through illness. Jack Corr (Erin's Own) failed to turn up at match venue. Dan Grace (Tullaroan) was subsequently awarded All-Ireland medal by the County Board.

1911

All-Ireland final not played. Kilkenny awarded title.

1912

November 17

Kilkenny 2-1 Cork 1-3

Jones' Road Sportsfield, Dublin

Attendance 18,000 (est.)

Kilkenny: John T Power (Piltown), Jack Keoghan (Tullaroan), Jack Rochford (Threecastles), Paddy 'Icy' Lannigan (Erin's Own), Dan Kennedy (Tullaroan), Dick 'Drooge' Walsh, captain (Mooncoin), Eddie Doyle (Mooncoin), Dick Doherty (Mooncoin), Matt Gargan (Erin's Own), Dick Grace (Tullaroan), Pierce Grace

(Tullaroan), John James Brennan (Erin's Own), Sim Walton, captain (Tullaroan), Dick Doyle (Mooncoin), Tom McCormack (Erin's Own), Jimmy 'The Wren' Kelly (Mooncoin), Mick Doyle (Mooncoin).

Subs: Denny Brennan (Dicksboro), Tom Dunne (Tullaroan), Jack Lennon (Erin's Own), Mick Nugent (Dicksboro), Pat Walsh (Threecastles).

1913
November 13
Kilkenny 2-4 Tipperary 1-2
Croke Park, Dublin
Attendance 20,000 (est.)

Kilkenny (13-a-side): John T Power (Piltown), Jack Keoghan (Tullaroan), Jack Rochford (Threecastles), Jack Lennon (Erin's Own), Dan Kennedy (Tullaroan), Dick 'Drooge' Walsh, captain (Mooncoin), Dick Grace (Tullaroan), John James Brennan (Erin's Own), Matt Gargan (Erin's Own), Pierce Grace (Tullaroan), Sim Walton (Tullaroan), Dick Dowling (Mooncoin), Dick Doyle (Mooncoin), Jimmy 'The Wren' Kelly (Mooncoin), Mick Doyle (Mooncoin).

Subs: Denny Brennan (Dicksboro), Joe Delahunty (Mooncoin), Paddy 'Icy' Lannigan (Erin's Own), Mick Quinn (Mooncoin), Jim Ryan (Mooncoin), Martin Ryan (Mooncoin), Jack Walsh (Threecastles).

Holohan

John Holohan, a 31-year-old farmer from Grangefertagh in Johnstown, wore the No.3 shirt in the 1922 All-Ireland final against Tipperary which, due to political and military matters, was not played until September, 1923. (Back row of team photo, fourth from left.)

chapter 2

Following the All-Ireland success in 1913, Kilkenny's Championship fortunes dipped dramatically. Over the following eight campaigns Kilkenny won only the 1916 provincial title. During those fallow years Kilkenny's decline was marked by five successive defeats by Dublin. No doubt, a myriad reasons were put forward to explain Kilkenny's prolonged lack of success, but perhaps the most compelling explanation was the County Board's inability to successfully complete separate senior Championships from 1916 onwards.

The 1916 Championship commenced in October but was not completed until August 1919, in what became known as 'The Triple Final', following the County Board decision to incorporate that 1916 county final with the finals of 1917 and 1918. The 1919 Championship was played but not finished as both finalists, Mooncoin and Tullaroan, were expelled for failing to agree on when and where to play the final. Due to the ongoing political and military upheaval that swept the country, there were no senior Championships in 1920, 1921 and 1922. Clearly during those years of senior inactivity the players' hurling skills, physical fitness and match sharpness would have dipped considerably, leaving them at a distinct disadvantage when on inter-county duty. By the onset of the summer of 1922 security matters had improved sufficiently to enable the players to engage in local practise games to hone their skills and fitness levels.

However, when Kilkenny set out against Laois in the opening game of that year's Championships, one suspects that, given the team's experiences over recent years, their ambitions were appropriately modest. Full-back on that team was John Holohan, a 31-year-old farmer from Grangefertagh in Johnstown.

John Holohan was born in 1891 to Johnny and Mary Holohan, formerly Connolly, from Cullahill, Co Laois. The Holohans were farmers, a life's calling that has been continued down the years at Grangefertagh, to the present owner Sean Holohan, Johnny and Mary's grandson.

Johnny and Mary Holohan had two sons, Paddy and John. Of the two boys only John demonstrated any interest in, or aptitude for, sport. From an early age he excelled at cricket and hurling, games equally popular in the locality. Despite the economic hardships and unfavourable political climate of the time, John found time to develop his hurling skills to such an extent that, by his 19th year, he was playing senior club hurling. His first notable hurling adventure was in helping local parish team, Crosspatrick, to the 1910 county semi-final.

—⚉—

By 1912 John was playing in the colours of another parish team, Johnstown. In the autumn of that year he had the distinction of playing in Johnstown's last 17-a-side game, an exhibition match against Mooncoin to celebrate the re-opening of St James' Park, Kilkenny. When Johnstown won the 1914 county Championship, John had accomplished his first major success. For that campaign Johnstown had availed of Tullaroan's internal difficulties by enlisting a number of their more prominent players, such as Sim Walton, Dick Grace, Dan Kennedy, Ger Doheny, and 'Fox' Maher. That John, though then only 23 years old, captained a team that included so many household names, confirmed his status as a quality hurler in his own right.

John was first selected for Kilkenny in February, 1915, for the semi-final of the Wolf Tone Tournament, then a very prestigious competition. Two other Johnstown players, Jim Byrne and Jim Harte, also made their inter-county debuts in that game. From the centre-back position, John won his first provincial title in November, 1916, when Wexford were routed on an 11-3 to 2-2 scoreline. The regrettable withdrawal of Jack Rochford, Paddy Donoghue and the Doyle brothers from the team prior to the All-Ireland final against Tipperary seriously hampered the team's chances and it was no real surprise that the game was lost by eight points. To quote *The Kilkenny People* on the matter: "Kilkenny were minus a few of their best players who disappointed at the last moment."

John would have to wait a further seven years to again sample the atmosphere of All-Ireland Sunday. In the meantime, the failure to win even a further provincial title over the following five Championships must have sown doubts in John's mind that he was ever destined to win that elusive All-Ireland medal.

Meanwhile, John's club career continued with mixed results. For the 1915 Championship he had transferred to Tullaroan, with whom he played throughout the rest of his career. Tullaroan won that year's Championship, defeating Dicksboro in the final. Thereafter, John's club career would be notable more for what he missed out on than for what he achieved. We have already noted the incidence of 'The Triple Final', that the 1919 county final was not played and that there were no Championships in 1920, 1921 and 1922. Thus, through no fault of his own, John was denied the opportunity to challenge for six separate Championships in those turbulent, unpredictable years.

However, John's perseverance was rewarded when, following the resumption of the Championship in 1923, Tullaroan, with John aboard, won successive titles in 1924 and 1925, defeating Clomanto and Dicksboro, respectively. Kilkenny, with John then playing at full-back, began the 1922 Championship with a comprehensive 5-5 to 1-2 win over Laois. The semi-final game against Wexford proved more difficult to arrange than to win, the game having to be postponed on four occasions – this difficulty in arranging the game was only to be expected, given the political climate of the time. When eventually played on November 3, Kilkenny cruised to a 5-6 to a 1 goal win to set up a Leinster final clash with Dublin on November 19. With five successive Championship defeats by Dublin to avenge Kilkenny were under enormous pressure going into that game, but, after an enthralling hour's hurling, they emerged winners on a 3-4 to 1-2 scoreline.

Political and military matters then intervened causing the All-Ireland final against Tipperary to be postponed until September, 1923. When the fixture was eventually confirmed Kilkenny commenced a training routine described as 'collective training', first established for the 1913 final.

The practice involved the players assembling at selected locations for two weeks of twice-daily intensive sessions, usually in St James' Park and Mooncoin. The publicity leading up to the game was very concentrated, the media responding to the sporting public's thirst for sports news and gossip, luxuries largely denied them during the years of the troubles.

Even the gentry got caught up in the pre-match build-up. In its eve-of-the-game edition *The Kilkenny People* reported that the team had been guests of the Earl of Ossory at Kilkenny Castle, and that they had also been entertained to tea by the Dowager, Countess of Desart, at her gardens at Aut Even. In its preview of the game, the same paper, in its reference to John, noted that, "John Holohan is fitted by nature for the responsible full-back position".

An attendance of over 26,000, paying record receipts of IR£24,355, witnessed a tremendously entertaining and exciting game, with Kilkenny emerging winners by a 4-2 to 2-6 margin. Two late goals from Paddy Donoghue and Dick Tobin denied Tipperary a win that, for long periods, looked the more likely outcome. One suspects that, when John and his comrades left Croke Park that memorable afternoon, little did they suspect that a further 44 Championship campaigns would run their course before another Kilkenny team would again defeat Tipperary in a senior final.

The Kilkenny People's match report was, understandably, fulsome in its praise of the team's achievement. It remarked that, "the game will rank as one of the greatest hurling contests in the history of the Association. Excitement ran high, but despite the stern nature of the struggle it was decided in a fine spirit. Kilkenny's display excelled in its brilliance any of the most outstanding displays of their illustrious predecessors." Sadly Dick Tobin, the scorer of Kilkenny's fourth goal, subsequently lost his life in a road accident in New York in 1953, where he had resided following his emigration shortly after the final.

Newspaper reports of the game were generous in their praise of the performance of Dick Grace, the only Kilkenny player remaining from the 1913 All-Ireland win over Tipperary. Mattie Power, John Roberts and John Holohan were also credited with outstanding displays. Thus, after years of sterling, but largely unrewarding, service to his county, John had finally achieved his goal. He won further Leinster titles in 1923 and 1925, but defeats by Galway both years in the All-Ireland semi-final thwarted his further All-Ireland ambitions.

The National Hurling League was inaugurated in the 1925–26 season. Cork were the competition's first winners, with Kilkenny winning only one of its six games to finish second bottom in the table.

John played in Kilkenny's two pre-Christmas League games, where a win over Tipperary and a defeat to Laois were registered.

On the League's resumption in the spring of 1926, he played in only two of Kilkenny's games, defeats to Galway and Cork. That Cork game at St James' Park in April was the last time followers saw John on active inter-county duty.

Sadly, John's last association with Kilkenny ended in controversial circumstances for which he was not responsible. He was selected on the panel for Kilkenny's final National League game against Limerick in May. Though John attended the game he did not tog out as he did not expect he would be used. His failure to do so subsequently became the subject matter of a bitter dispute between the Tullaroan club and the County Chairman, Tom Walsh, concerning the latter's comments on John's actions. Seamus Byrne, *The Kilkenny People*'s chief sports writer, was also drawn into the dispute as it was his reporting of the County Chairman's original remarks that first set the dispute in motion.

—⚍—

John retired from inter-county hurling prior to the commencement of that year's Championship. His decision was not connected to the fall-out from the Limerick game. He was, by then, in his 35th year and had served his county bravely since his debut, in February 1915.

John's last club Championship game was in June, 1926, in Tullaroan's first-round defeat by Mooncoin, played at Waterford before an attendance of over 8,000. In its report of the game, *The Kilkenny People* remarked: "John Holohan was safe throughout, but the years are beginning to tell on him."

Sadly, John had retired before the inauguration of the inter-provincial Championships in 1927. Had this competition been in vogue during his career John would, no doubt, have earned inter-provincial representation.

Sean Holohan recalls his father maintaining a keen interest in hurling throughout his life and remembers him travelling to all the important Championship games, by train if to Croke Park, or by bicycle if to Kilkenny or Thurles. However, recalls Sean: "My father rarely spoke about his own hurling achievements. He was simply not the type to engage in self-praise. His main passion was in farming and he would spend most of his leisure hours discussing all the farming issues of the day with neighbouring farmers."

"My father never expressed much interest in politics or related matters," Sean further revealed, "possibly due to having lived through the troubled 1916-1923 period when people's ordinary lives were so affected. However, if pressed on the matter he would have been a pro-Treaty supporter."

John's career was marked by the usual mix of elation and despair associated with lengthy sporting careers. His calm nature allowed him to put both his achievements and disappointments aside and to move forward to the next set of challenges. He played the game he loved for the sheer enjoyment of it, but also with the required level of commitment and determination to enable him to do himself and his team justice. He played at a time when pursuing a sport with such nationalistic and cultural connotations was extremely difficult given the prevailing unforgiving political climate. The harsh economic conditions of the time would also have impacted on pursuing most leisure-related activities.

John died in June, 1947, following a short illness. The family were very honoured that most of his comrades from the 1922 team attended his funeral. He was survived by his wife, Ellen, and his four children, Sean, Mary, Sheila and Hilda. Sean works the family farm at Grangefertagh, where he resides with his wife Mary and family.

That 1922 win was one of Kilkenny's most significant of all their All-

Ireland wins. It broke Kilkenny's nine-year losing sequence. It helped to consolidate Kilkenny as a hurling county, and maintained its record of winning a senior title at least once every decade since that inaugural win of 1904, a record that holds to date. That the win was against arch rivals Tipperary only added to its lustre. If, for no other reason, Kilkenny followers will forever acclaim the hurling life of John Holohan.

CAREER HIGHLIGHTS

All-Ireland senior finalist: 1916 and 1922
All-Ireland senior winner: 1922
Leinster senior winner: 1916, 1922, 1923 and 1925
County senior winner: 1914 (Johnstown); 1915, 1924 and 1925 (Tullaroan)

ALL-IRELAND WINNING TEAMS

1922

September 9, 1923
Kilkenny 4-2 Tipperary 2-6
Croke Park, Dublin
Attendance 26,000 (est.)

Kilkenny: Mark McDonald (Clonmore), Jimmy Tobin (Clomanto), John Holohan (Tullaroan), Pat Glendon (Clomanto), Tommy Carroll (Clonmore), Wattie Dunphy, captain (Clonmore), Dick Grace (Tullaroan), Pat 'Dexter'Aylward (Knockmoylan), Bill Kenny (Ballyraggett), Martin 'Roundy' Lalor (Threecastles), Eddie Dunphy (Mooncoin), Paddy O'Donoghue (Dicksboro), Dick Tobin (Clomanto), John Roberts (Dicksboro), Mattie Power (Dicksboro).

Subs: Bill Brennan (Clomanto), Mick Brennan (Clomanto), Tim Scott (Galmoy), Tom Tierney (Callan).

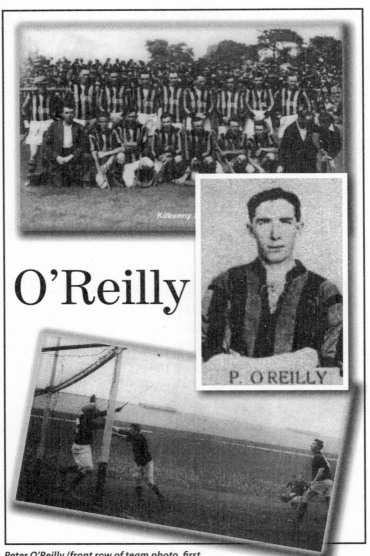

O'Reilly

Peter O'Reilly (front row of team photo, first
player on left), a 24 year-old from Dicksboro, met with
disappointment in an All-Ireland final before helping Kilkenny to
three titles – the county's 9th, 10th and 11th – in the mid-'30s.
He is pictured in action (far right) against Cork in the 1931 All-
Ireland final.

chapter 3

The vacancy caused by John Holohan's retirement in 1925 was filled almost as soon as it arose. The selectors turned to Peter O'Reilly, a 24-year-old from the Dicksboro club. Peter had demonstrated himself to be a hurler of immense potential in his club's Championship campaign of 1925, which concluded in a county final defeat to Tullaroan. Despite that set-back it was evident that Peter's career was on rise. In relation to hurling skill, physical make-up, athleticism and temperament, Peter had them in abundance. He seemed ideally suited to meet the many challenges that playing inter-county hurling would present, especially in the physically taxing position of full-back.

The selectors' faith in Peter would, in time, be richly rewarded. Over the following decade he carved out a career in which he won every honour available to him, and became one of the outstanding full-backs of his own, or any, era.

Peter made his inter-county debut on March 28, 1926, in Kilkenny's National League defeat to Dublin at St James' Park. He missed Kilkenny's Leinster semi-final win over Dublin (Wattie Dunphy deputised), but was present when Kilkenny defeated Offaly in the Leinster final. He had won the first of many honours that marked his career .

In relation to Kilkenny's 6-5 to 5-1 win over Galway in the All-Ireland semi-final, *The Kilkenny People* noted: "O'Reilly saved the day on many occasions, and handled the ball safely throughout. He appears to have a great career in front of him. He is the right man in the right place and, with experience, he should achieve great things for Kilkenny."

Like his full-back predecessors, Jack Rochford and John Holohan, Peter would first have to endure All-Ireland final disappointment before winning the game's highest honour, as Kilkenny proved no match for Cork in that year's All-Ireland final. After trailing by only a point at half time (2-1 to 2-0) Kilkenny failed to score in the second-half and were eventually defeated by a margin of 12 points.

The remaining years of the decade were barren ones for both Peter and Kilkenny, with Dublin securing the 1927 and 1928 Leinster titles. The 1929 hurling year was to prove a turbulent one for Kilkenny, as well as Peter and his club. The Dicksboro club were in dispute with the County Board regarding team selection policy. In support of the club's stance, Peter and some of Dicksboro's other county players did not play any Championship hurling that year for Kilkenny. As matters transpired, Kilkenny did win the Leinster Championship but, following an objection by Dublin, both teams were subsequently expelled from the Championship, which was then declared void. Despite that expulsion, Kilkenny were, on an 8 to 7 majority, nominated by the Leinster Council to represent the province in the All-Ireland semi-final against Galway. That there were doubts, as to whether had Kilkenny defeated Galway they would be permitted to play the All-Ireland final, appeared to have an adverse effect on their commitment to the game, which they lost convincingly, following a very dispirited performance.

The difficulties between Dicksboro and the County Board were, subsequently, partially resolved enabling Peter to play in the latter stages of the 1929–1930 National League. However, when Kilkenny sensationally lost the 1930 Leinster semi-final to Laois, Peter was again absent. Whether this absence was due to injury, or was a carry over from the previous year's troubles is unclear. What may be significant is that Dicksboro's other high-profile players, John Roberts and Podge Byrne, were also unexplained absentees. In its match report, *The Kilkenny People* was very critical of the Kilkenny forward line. It noted: "To say that they were hopeless would be a mild expression. They were anything but a forward line. Any six forwards selected should have some knowledge of the whereabouts of the posts." The reporter subsequently exonerated newcomer Paddy Phelan from any responsibility for the defeat. Phelan was later to become one of the greatest wing backs the game has known, his selection on the 'Team of the Century' being unchallenged.

The same newspaper unequivocally rebuked the Dicksboro club for its attitude towards the county team, remarking that, in the newspaper's view, the club had always been fairly and proportionally represented on Kilkenny teams.

With all internal difficulties resolved, Kilkenny faced the 1931 Championship at full strength. A 4-7 to 4-2 win over Laois in the Leinster final gave Kilkenny its first provincial title since 1926. Having comfortably defeated Galway in the semi-final Kilkenny then faced Cork in the All-Ireland final. One suspects that no member of either team was prepared for the series of events that followed, events that would propel them and the game of hurling to a level of public esteem hitherto unknown in Gaelic games. It took three enthralling contests before Cork emerged as winners of their 11th title. By then, Cork were an experienced, but also an ageing, team, and a further 10 years would elapse before their next title win.

The draw and two replays were played before a combined attendance of 91,519, which represented an exceptional response by supporters, considering the unforgiving economic, and travelling, conditions of the time. That the game's had captivated the attention of the hurling public, both new and old, is evident in the attendances of 33,124 and 31,985 at the first and second replays, despite both games being played at the onset of winter.

Apart from the attraction of the games themselves, the unprecedented publicity they received from the national media helped enormously to sharpen the supporters' insatiable appetite towards all things hurling. The fledging *Irish Press* newspaper, backed by the Fianna Fail party, was the first of the national dailies to afford the games the level of exposure that, in these days, is taken for granted, but at that time was not considered either economically profitable or politically expedient. Thereafter, all national daily newspapers competed vigorously for the expanding Gaelic games market, a situation that prevails to this day.

Notwithstanding the fanfare and enthusiasm surrounding the trilogy of games, the harsh reality for Peter to absorb was that a second All-Ireland final defeat had been visited on him. Kilkenny's best opportunities to win had occurred in the first draw and first replay, Cork drawing level both days with late points. The second replay saw Kilkenny fielding a much depleted team, with Lory Meagher, Paddy Larkin and Dick Morrissey all absent through injury. Nonetheless, it took a late scoring blitz by Cork to bring the series to a conclusion.

Successful sports people are, in the main, a very resilient and flexible breed, possessing that unique ability to consign victories and defeats to history before moving on to the next series of challenges This dexterity of mind and body was to stand the men of 1931 in good stead over the following four Championship campaigns, of which they would win three.

Peter broke his All-Ireland final losing sequence the following year when Kilkenny edged out Clare in a tough, uncompromising game, winning by a three-point margin (3-3 to 2-3). The surge of interest in hurling which 'The Triple Final' of the previous year had generated was continued when a new All-Ireland final attendance record was set with 34,372 patrons present.

Since the beginning of the century, Kilkenny's toughest opponents were invariably Cork and Tipperary. With both these counties then about to enter parallel periods of decline a new force emerged from Munster in the form of Limerick. Kilkenny and Limerick would engage in many memorable games during the 1930s, in both National League and Championship. Their rivalry was first established in the National League final in 1933, which Kilkenny won. They next met in that year's All-Ireland final when, before a new attendance record of 45,176, Kilkenny successfully defended their 1932 title by a four point margin (1-7 to 0-6) in a game that is generally regarded as being the first of the 'Classic Finals'. In its match report *The Kilkenny People* noted that, "Peter O Reilly and Podge Byrne formed an impenetrable defensive line in the Kilkenny backline".

The 1934 Championship had presented Kilkenny with a realistic opportunity to achieve the county's second three-in-a-row of All-Ireland titles. Curiously, and fatally as it transpired, Kilkenny undertook a gruelling six-week tour of the East Coast of America between their Leinster semi-final win over Laois and the provincial final. Their inevitable defeat in that game was heavily criticised by a section of Kilkenny followers who questioned the wisdom of undertaking such an arduous tour when history beckoned.

Limerick won the League-Championship double in 1934, to cement their standing as Kilkenny's main rivals. Thus, when the counties met in the 1935 All-Ireland final, it was no surprise that a new attendance record for a final in either code of 46,591 was set. Despite the appalling, energy-sapping wet conditions, the teams went head-to-head in an absorbing game. Once again Kilkenny emerged winners by the tightest of margins (2-5 to 2-4). Their defence was under severe pressure in the closing minutes as Limerick attacked relentlessly to salvage the game. The Kilkenny full-back line of Paddy Larkin, Peter and Peter Blanchfield were especially praised for their defensive work in those hectic closing minutes as Kilkenny held out to secure its 11th title. In its match report, *The Kilkenny People* noted that, "Peter O'Reilly held McMahon, Limerick's full-forward in total subjugation, displaying great powers of anticipation in his approach and by his generally fine hurling drew the applause of his admirers." Peter was now a triple All-Ireland winner.

Within twelve months, Peter was back in Croke Park in pursuit of further honours. Kilkenny uniquely fielded the same 15 players that had won the previous year, but there the similarities ended as Limerick reversed that result by a 13-point margin (5-6 to 1-5). Once again the appeal of both teams was reflected in another All-Ireland final record attendance of 51,235. Peter retired from inter-county hurling shortly afterwards with a fifty percent success ratio, a ratio he would probably have accepted back in 1931 following that year's defeat.

Peter had the distinction of winning the county's first National League title in 1933. That Kilkenny would not again win the League until 1962 illustrates the rarity of the county's success in the competition.

When the Inter-Provincial Championships for the Railway Cups were launched in 1927 they became an instant success, with players and followers alike. Players regarded inter-provincial selection as a great honour, and a Railway Cup medal ranked second only to an All-Ireland medal in prestige. When Leinster won the inaugural final, Peter was substitute full-back, a significant honour in itself, considering he had only one year's inter-county experience behind him. He was full-back in Leinster's back-to-back wins in 1932 and 1933. Injury in the early weeks of 1936 prevented Peter playing in

Leinster's title win, his place being taken by his club mate, Podge Byrne.

At club level, Peter played throughout his career with Dicksboro, a display of loyalty to his first club that was in stark contrast to that of many of his inter-county colleagues, who, in the absence of a 'Parish Rule' moved freely between clubs. This unrestricted movement of players was clearly injurious to the fortunes of the junior clubs, who invariably found themselves deprived of their best players. The County Board saw the situation differently in that the system gave the better junior players an opportunity to play at the higher grade and gain more exposure to the county's senior selectors. Peter played in four county finals, winning in 1926, but losing in 1925, 1928 and 1937.

During his playing days Peter turned to refereeing, a practice that was not uncommon at the time amongst high-profile, inter-county players. He refereed the county senior finals of 1932, 1935 and 1938. Peter's passion for sport also found outlets in other areas. He was an accomplished handballer and had considerable success at club level. Having always had a keen interest in greyhounds, Peter ultimately became a successful breeder, working with his brother, Ken.

Though in failing health for some time, Peter's death in February 1940 came as a major shock to the community and the county. He was a few months short of his 38th birthday, his death coming a year and some months after he refereed his last county final. Such was the impact of his death, that, in a break with tradition, Kilkenny Corporation suspended its Standing Orders to allow its members pay tribute to Peter. Speaker after speaker referred to Peter's talent as a hurler, his loyalty to his club and his community, noting that he had been an outstanding ambassador for the city and the county.

That Peter was one of the game's most accomplished full-backs is beyond dispute. He soldiered heroically on the edge of the square for club, county and province throughout his career, one in which he encountered the game's most celebrated forwards. He became Kilkenny's third All-Ireland winning full-back and, in so doing, set a very daunting standard for his successor.

Peter was born on September 29, 1902, and died on February 25, 1940. He was a baker by trade, spending all his working life at Mulhall's Bakery, Green St. He never married.

CAREER HIGHLIGHTS

All-Ireland senior finalists: 1926, 1931(3), 1932, 1933, 1935 and 1936

All-Ireland senior winner: 1932, 1933 and 1935

Leinster senior winner: 1926, 1931, 1932, 1933, 1935 and 1936

County senior finalist: 1925, 1926, 1928 and 1937

County senior winner: 1926

National League winner: 1932/33

Railway Cup winner: 1927(s), 1932 and 1933. Missed 1936 win through injury.

ALL-IRELAND WINNING TEAMS

1932

September 4

Kilkenny 3-3 Clare 2-3

Croke Park

Attendance 34,372

Kilkenny: Jim Dermody (Tullaroan), Paddy Larkin (Tullaroan), Peter O'Reilly (Dicksboro), Jack 'Sag' Carroll (Dicksboro), Paddy Phelan (Tullaroan), Podge Byrne (Dicksboro), Eddie Doyle (Mooncoin), Lory Meagher (Tullaroan), Eddie Byrne (Young Ireland, Dublin), Jimmy Walsh, captain (Carrickshock), Martin Power (Army Metropolitan, Dublin), Tommy Leahy (Urlingford), Dan Dunne (Young Irelands, Dublin), Martin White (Tullaroan), Mattie Power (Garda, Dublin).

Sub: Billy Dalton (Carrickshock), Paddy Dowling (Dicksboro), Jack Duggan (Mooncoin), John Fitzpatrick (Carrickshock), Jim Grace (Garda, Dublin), Bill 'Dux' Kelly (Carrickshock), Jimmy O'Connell (Dicksboro).

1933

September 3

Kilkenny 1-7 Limerick 0-6

Croke Park

Attendance 45,176

Kilkenny: Jim Dermody (Tullaroan), Paddy Larkin (Tullaroan), Peter O'Reilly (Dicksboro), Eddie Doyle, captain (Mooncoin), Paddy Phelan (Tullaroan), Podge Byrne (Dicksboro), Tommy Leahy (Young Irelands, Dublin), Eddie Byrne (Young Irelands, Dublin), Lory Meagher (Tullaroan), Jimmy Walsh (Carrickshock), Martin Power (Army Metropolitan, Dublin), Martin White (Tullaroan), John Fitzpatrick (Carrickshock), Johnny Dunne (Mooncoin), Mattie Power (Garda, Dublin).

Sub: Jack 'Sag' Carroll (Dicksboro), Dan Dunne (Young Irelands, Dublin), Jack Duggan (Mooncoin), replaced White (injured 45 mins), Jim Grace (Garda, Dublin), Tommy Grace (Tullaroan), Jimmy O'Connell (Dicksboro) replaced Dermody (injured 59 mins), John O'Farrell (Carrickshock).

1935

September 1

Kilkenny 2-5, Limerick 2-4

Croke Park

Attendance 46,591

Kilkenny: Jimmy O'Connell (Dicksboro), Paddy Larkin (James Stephens), Peter O'Reilly (Dicksboro), Peter Blanchfield (James Stephens), Eddie Byrne (Young Ireland, Dublin), Podge Byrne (Dicksboro), Paddy Phelan (Tullaroan), Tommy Leahy (Young Ireland, Dublin), Lory Meagher (Tullaroan), Jimmy Walsh (Carrickshock), Jack Duggan (Mooncoin), Martin White (Tullaroan), Johnny Dunne (Mooncoin), Loughlin 'Locky' Byrne (Mooncoin), Mattie Power (Garda, Dublin).

Sub: Jim Dermody (Tullaroan), Paddy Kealy (Young Irelands, Dublin), Mick Tyrell (James Stephens), Jack Phelan (Carrickshock), Larry Duggan (Mooncoin) replaced Dunne (injured 10 mins) who replaced Jack Duggan (injured half-time), Mick Larkin (James Stephens), Jimmy Purcell (Dicksboro), Billy Burke (Tullaroan), Lar Carroll (James

Stephens), Willie Dunphy (Mooncoin), Jimmy Kelly (Carrickshock), Milo Kennedy (Tullaroan), Frank Minogue (Carrickshock), Paddy Obbins (Dicksboro).

Kilkenny SH 1939

Larkin

James Stephens' Paddy Larkin won four All-Ireland medals, but wore the No.3 shirt with distinction in the infamous 'Thunder and Lightning' final against Cork, in 1939. He proudly wears his cap, kneeling fourth from right on the front row of this 1939 photo. Interestingly, Jack Rochford is pictured in the same photo, on the right in the back row.

chapter 4

Of Kilkenny's 14 All-Ireland winning full-backs, none had as disappointing a Championship debut and an equally disappointing Championship finale as Paddy Larkin. He made that first appearance in Portlaoise in July, 1930, where a very dispirited Kilkenny side were sensationally defeated by Laois in the provincial semi-final. Roll on a further 13 summers to Belfast, in 1943, where Paddy, then the team's most experienced player, was helpless in preventing Antrim cause one of hurling's greatest-ever Championship upsets, defeating Kilkenny by three points in the All-Ireland semi-final (3-3 to 1-6).

If the book-end years of Paddy's career are less than memorable, the intervening ones were distinctly otherwise, during which time he became a serial winner of all hurling's major honours. He mastered the dark world of full-back-line defending and became one of the game's outstanding and popular characters. He was at the height of his powers during the 1930s, winning All-Ireland medals in 1932, 1933, 1935 and 1939.

Paddy was one of eight children of Philip and Johanna Larkin (formerly Walsh) of Kells Road, Kilkenny. He had one sister, Mary, and six brothers, Mick (Phleep) an All-Ireland winner with Kilkenny, John, Philly, Jim and Ned, all of whom played with James Stephens. Sadly, a brother, Martin, died young.

Paddy's introduction to competitive hurling began with the De La Salle school's team which competed in city leagues. In time, he graduated to the James Stephens adult team, then performing at junior level. Paddy's first major success came in 1924 when James Stephens, founded in 1887, won the county Championship, the club's first such win in any grade. While Paddy played in a tournament game for the county senior team in early 1926, he was not retained for that year's Championship. He did, however, play Championship hurling that year with the county junior team. While based for a time in The Curragh as a member of the Defence Forces, Paddy won a number of Army hurling titles.

The closing stages of the 1927 senior Championship was Paddy's initial major hurling adventure. James Stephens and Mooncoin had qualified for the county final but, as the semi-finals had not been played until late November, it was decided to hold over the final until early the following year. Thus, on January 27, James Stephens won on a 4-2 to 3-2 scoreline. However, due to the post-match controversy surrounding a late Mooncoin 'goal' which was disallowed, James Stephens agreed to a replay, which took place on March 4. Mooncoin won that game, but, following an objection by James Stephens, the County Board ordered a further replay. This game took place in Waterford on August 19, but had to be abandoned due to unplayable weather conditions. The saga was finally concluded on September 23, again at Waterford, where Mooncoin took the title on a 2-4 to 2-2 scoreline. Not for the only time in his career would Paddy end on a losing side in a marathon hurling final.

James Stephens did not contest a county final again until 1935. In the interim there were some dark days for Paddy and his club. In 1930, through an unusual set of circumstances, the club thought that they had reached the county final despite not having played a single Championship match. They had received a bye in the first round and were drawn to play the winners of Carrickshock-Dicksboro in the semi-final. However, when both of those clubs were expelled from the Championship, on breaches of player registration rules [a euphemism for playing illegal players] James Stephens thought that the way was clear for them to contest the final. Their apparent good fortune soon dissipated when the County Board rearranged the semi-final pairings, to which decision the club reacted by refusing to play their game against Urlingford, and were duly expelled. In 1931, the club qualified for the county semi-final, but an internal dispute was largely responsible for their heavy defeat by Urlingford. For the following three Championship campaigns, Paddy played with Tullaroan, while James Stephens struggled just to survive.

Despite his relative inactivity with his club in 1930, Paddy was selected for the county team for the latter stages of the 1929-30 National League. He held his place for the Championship, making his debut in that ill-fated game against Laois. While the defeat was not the type of Championship opening he would have wished for, Paddy would have gained some personal satisfaction from *The Kilkenny People* match report, which noted that, "Paddy Larkin distinguished himself in the right corner and played splendidly". That provincial semi-final defeat would not be repeated again during Paddy's career, as Kilkenny qualified for every provincial final while he was on duty.

With wins over Wexford, Meath and Laois, a re-energised Kilkenny won the 1931 provincial title, giving Paddy the first of his nine Leinster medals. A comfortable win over Galway in the semi-final, paved the way for Kilkenny's All-Ireland final challenge to Munster champions, Cork. History reveals that Cork emerged winners after three absorbing games, games that captured the attention of hurling followers, as no final had hitherto. While hurling in general was the ultimate winner, the harsh reality for Paddy was that, despite being marginally the better team in the first draw and first replay, Kilkenny had failed to secure the win. To add to Paddy's woes, he was forced to miss the second replay through injury.

For the remaining years of the decade, Paddy and Kilkenny were rarely out of the limelight. The Leinster Championship was retained and, following a titanic struggle, Kilkenny edged out Clare in the 1932 All-Ireland final, to secure their ninth title.

That the win was highly acclaimed within the county is evident from *The Kilkenny People*'s passionate match report which began as follows: "Welcome to our All-Ireland champions. Welcome to the greatest hurlers that ever wielded a caman. The memories of a decade ago, memories buried in the misty recesses of the past have been resurrected. The vista of ten long years of patient waiting have been rolled back."

Paddy was back in Croke Park within 12 months collecting his second All-Ireland title, as Kilkenny confirmed their earlier National League final win, over Limerick by again outscoring Mick Mackey's men in a high-quality game.

Kilkenny aspirations to successfully defend their titles in 1934 were almost certainly derailed by their ill-timed American tour, following their Leinster semi-final win. Events over the following 12 months would indicate that the tour's critics had valid grounds for their opinions as, in the 1934–35 National League, which was run on a points system, Limerick finishing league champions with 15 points to Kilkenny's 14 points. Despite that avoidable loss of their Leinster title it was clear that Kilkenny were still Limerick's main threat.

That newly established rivalry between Kilkenny and Limerick, both on and off the field, was such that an All-Ireland final clash between them was almost demanded by the hurling public. Kilkenny's reputation was well established, while Limerick's valiant efforts in 1933, and victory in 1934, together with their back-to-back National League titles of 1934 and 1935, had captivated the attention of all hurling followers. Thus, when the counties faced each other in the 1935 All-Ireland final, a record attendance of 46,591 was present. Despite the extremely difficult playing conditions, the game developed into a real thriller, with Kilkenny emerging as winners by a solitary point. For Paddy the dark days of 1930 and 1931 were comprehensively banished as he became a triple All-Ireland medal winner. In its match report, *The Kilkenny People* noted that, "Larkin was in determined mood, playing a brilliant defensive game. He gave his marker, Clohessy, the toughest day of his career."

Paddy's next two attempts at winning a fourth title came badly unstuck. In 1936 a new record All-Ireland final attendance, in either code, of 51,235 saw Limerick comprehensively reverse the previous year's result on a 5-6 to 1-5 scoreline. To add to Paddy's disappointment, he was Kilkenny's captain that forgettable day.

The following year saw a Kilkenny team, that was clearly over the hill, demolished by Tipperary on a 3-11 to 0-3 score line, the county's worst All-Ireland final defeat since 1893. The concerns widely held around the county, that the selectors had failed to learn the lessons from the Limerick mauling of 1936, were again ventilated as a youthful Tipperary coasted to victory, having led at half time by 2-8 to 0-2. Paddy's bad luck as county captain was repeated in 1938 when Kilkenny lost the Leinster final to Dublin, following a replay.

The defeats of the previous three years, together with the retirement of most of the team's long-serving players, opened the door to a new generation of emerging hurlers. Thus, when Kilkenny set out on the Championship trail in 1939, eight of the successful minor team of 1935 were on the panel. Having regained the Leinster title, and defeated Galway in the semi-final, Kilkenny faced Cork in the All-Ireland final. The unfamiliarity of both teams with the many and diverse challenges that All-Ireland Sunday would present, did not inhibit them serving up a classic, despite the dreadful weather conditions. Paddy, Jimmy Walsh and Paddy Phelan were the only survivors of Kilkenny's successful 1932 team. Heavy rain in the morning and a miserable weather forecast kept attendance down to 39,302. While the game began in reasonably sunny weather, conditions worsened drastically to the extent that the majorty of the second half was played in a downpour, interspersed with thunder and lightning. The dark clouds that were sweeping Europe, as the initial salvos of the Second World War were fired, seemed to spread to Croke Park as the stadium was enveloped in semi-darkness. So difficult did the conditions become, and so restricted was visibility, that it was not until after the game that Kilkenny followers learned that the scorer of the winning point was midfielder, Jimmy Kelly. This 'thunder and lightning' final brought the successful 1930s to an appropriately clamorous conclusion.

That memorable win gave Paddy his fourth All-Ireland title. In relation to his performance, *The Kilkenny People* noted that, "Larkin at full-back was like a rock and kept his marker away from goalie, Jimmy O'Connell, who also had his best game of the year." Kilkenny's 1939 win put them level with Tipperary in the Roll of Honour with 12 titles each, one more than Cork. When one considers that both Tipperary and Cork had each won six titles before Kilkenny won its first in 1904, the milestone that the 1939 win marked is impressive by any standard.

Paddy's last appearance on All-Ireland Sunday ended in a loss to Limerick in the 1940 final. This was a game Kilkenny were expected to win as they fielded the same team that had won the previous year, while Limerick were regarded as a team well past its best. Kilkenny had the better of the opening half and led by 1-4 to 1-2 at the break. Limerick, with their iconic leader Mick Mackey dominating matters around midfield, then took control, emerging winners by a six point margin (3-7 to 1-7).

After that Limerick defeat, Kilkenny surprisingly went into a period of decline over the final three years of Paddy's career. The team's only success, the 1943 Leinster title, was quickly forgotten following their subsequent shock defeat by Antrim in the All-Ireland semi-final. That game marked Paddy's last competitive inter-county game. He quietly retired after14 year's sterling service to his county.

At inter-provincial level Paddy experienced considerable success, winning Railway Cup medals in 1932 (at right-half-back), 1933, and 1936 as captain. Injury forced him out of the 1941 final, which Leinster won.

Paddy won his only National League medal in 1933, Kilkenny's first-ever win in that competition. Due to war restrictions, which curtailed the supply of petrol, rubber and other transport-related items, the League was suspended during the final two years of his career, being replaced by a four-county league between Kilkenny, Wexford, Waterford and Tipperary.

Paddy won his sole Oireachtas Tournament medal in 1940, the second year of the competition's existence, a competition that would, in time, and for over 30 years, command a lofty place in the hurling calendar. Curiously, Kilkenny, with their full

All-Ireland winning team on duty, had been defeated by Limerick in the inaugural final of 1939.

At club level Paddy had the distinction of winning county Championships with three different clubs. For a very committed James Stephens man it was somewhat ironic that his first and second titles were won in the colours of Tullaroan. Previously referred to internal difficulties in James Stephens in 1931 carried over into the following year when the club did not participate in the Championship. To enable Paddy, his brother Mick, Peter Blanchfield and Paddy Walsh, to play senior club hurling, the County Board allowed them to transfer to Tullaroan, who won the 1933 and 1934 Championships with all four imports on board. When James Stephens resolved their differences and returned to senior ranks in 1935, Paddy captained them to that year's county title, the club's first at senior grade. He also captained the successful 1937 team. Paddy's fifth and last county title was won in the colours of Eire Og, a city-based club, sadly long since disbanded. He subsequently returned to James Stephens, playing his last Championship game in 1944, in their first round defeat by Mullinavat.

Paddy was one of hurling's outstanding defenders. He made light of his slight 5' 7" frame by playing with a determination and sense of competitiveness that was almost frightening. Allied to those qualities was an unquenchable mental strength. He brought an array of skills to the game that never failed him. His game was a cocktail of deft stick work, close marking, coolness under pressure and unquenchable courage. He was, simply, a miniature colossus of the game.

The Larkin family is one of the few GAA families to experience All-Ireland senior success through three generations. Paddy had the pleasure of seeing his son, Fan, replicate all of his own successes by winning copious All-Ireland, Leinster, National League, Railway Cup (also as captain) and county Championship titles in an equally stellar career. Paddy's grandson, Philip, is also an All-Ireland medallist at senior, Under-21, minor, club and colleges levels. Both Fan and Philly are All-Star winners.

Paddy, after retiring from Army service, spent the rest of his working life with Cleeres, a city-based building company. He was married to Anne McGuiness, with whom he had three sons, Fan, Paddy and Michael. Paddy Larkin, one of Kilkenny's and hurling's greatest exponents, died in 1976.

CAREER HIGHLIGHTS

All-Ireland senior finalist: 1931(2), 1932, 1933, 1935, 1936, 1937, 1939 and 1940
All-Ireland senior winner: 1932, 1933, 1935 and 1939.
Leinster senior winner: 1931, 1932, 1933, 1935, 1936, 1937, 1939, 1940 and 1943
National League winner: 1932/33
Railway Cup winner: 1932, 1933 and 1936 (c), missed 1941 win through injury
County senior Championship winner: 1933 and 1934, (Tullaroan), 1935 and 1937, (James Stephens), 1939, (Eire Og)
County junior Championship winner: 1924 (James Stephens)

Oireachtas Tournament winner: 1940

American tour: 1934

ALL-IRELAND WINNING TEAMS

1939
September 3
Kilkenny 2-7 Cork 3-3
Croke Park
Attendance 39,302

Kilkenny: Jimmy O'Connell (Dicksboro), Paddy Grace (James Stephens), Paddy Larkin (Eire Og), Peter Blanchfield (Tullaroan), Bobby Hinks (Carrickshock), Billy Burke (Tullaroan), Paddy Phelan (Tullaroan), Jimmy Kelly (Carrickshock), Jimmy Walsh, captain (Carrickshock), Jim Langton (Eire Og), Terry Leahy (Faughs, Dublin), Jack Gargan (Tullaroan), Jack Mulcahy (Eire Og), Seanie O'Brien (Eire Og), Jimmy Phelan (Tullaroan).

Sub: Bob Aylward (Carrickshock), Bobby Branigan (Dicksboro) replaced Gargan (injured half-time), Paddy O'Donovan (Carrickshock), Jim Malone (Carrickshock), Paddy Boyle (Eire Og), Paddy Shortall (James Stephens), Dinny Keane (Dicksboro).

Hayden

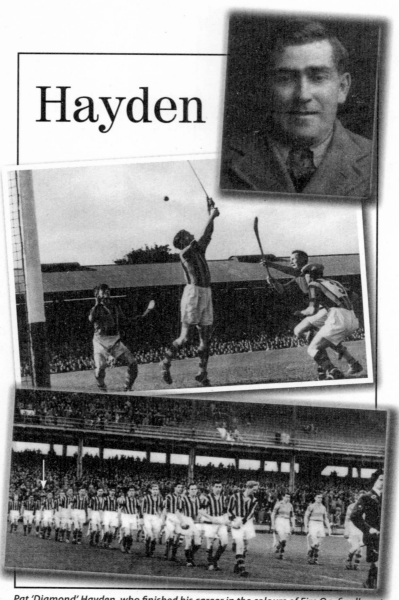

Pat 'Diamond' Hayden, who finished his career in the colours of Eire Og, finally got his chance to wear the Kilkenny No.3 jersey in his 30s. The main photo catches him, in his signature flat cap, keeping a close eye on future Taoiseach, Jack Lynch, in the 1947 All-Ireland final against Cork.
Bottom photo: Pat is towards the back of the line, indicated by the arrow, in the pre-match parade at the Oireachtas final, in 1951.

chapter 5

Pat 'Diamond' Hayden was born in the townland of Moonteenmore, in the parish of Gowran on March 26, 1916, to James and Anastasia Hayden. He had two brothers, Jack and Jim, and one sister, Biddy (Gardiner). Pat attended primary school at nearby Dungarvan National School, and there his initial hurling adventures commenced. He later played with the local Gowran minor team.

By the early to mid-1940s, Pat's hurling profile was modest by any standards. He had made his senior inter-county debut in April, 1945 in a Four Counties League game against Waterford. That competition was a mini-league involving Kilkenny, Waterford, Wexford and Tipperary, organised in substitution for the National League, which had been suspended in 1942 due to the shortage of petrol and other transport-related commodities brought about by the ongoing World War. He was not retained for that year's Championship.

At that time, Pat was playing club hurling on two fronts. At junior level he lined out with Castle Rovers, a team drawn from the Gowran, Clara, and Goresbridge area, and, at senior level, with 'The Northern' selection. That dual mandate arose following the County Board's decision in the early 1940s to allow divisional teams, comprising players from junior clubs, and two FCA teams, to compete in the senior Championship. This experiment, originally introduced in an attempt to spruce up a somewhat predictable senior Championship, was discontinued after a short trial period.

The game which reignited Pat's career was the 1945 county senior semi-final between 'The Northern' selection and Eire Og, the county champions whose forward line included players of the stature of Jim Langton, Jack Mulcahy and Jack Gargan. Almost single-handedly Pat kept his team in contention, the senior club only securing their narrow four-points win courtesy of a late scoring blitz. His display was duly noted in the local media and by hurling people around the county.

Thus, it was no surprise when the Kilkenny junior selectors chose Pat as full-back for the 1946 Championship. That team subsequently developed into a particularly strong combination, out-playing all opposition en route to becoming Leinster and All-Ireland champions. In the five games played the team scored an impressive 27 goals and 24 points, while conceding a mere eight goals and 15 points. As colleagues on that team Pat had a number of players who subsequently carved out very successful senior careers – such as Mark Marnell, Peter Prendergast, Mick Kenny, Shem Downey, Jack Egan and Bill Cahill who all repeated that junior success subsequently at senior level.

—m—

Following that junior All-Ireland win, Pat would have been forgiven if he had called time on his hurling commitments and slipped quietly into retirement. After all, he had his All-Ireland souvenir safely tucked away, and, not insignificantly, he was by then approaching his 31st birthday. Also, there did not appear to be any great need for his services by the senior selectors following the return to the county colours of the younger Mick Butler, after several successful years playing with Dublin. Butler, a member of a strong hurling family from Lismateige, Hugginstown, had played full back in Dublin's 1938 All-Ireland win, had won additional Leinster titles in 1941, 1942 and 1944, and was Leinster's full-back in their 1941 Railway Cup win. Clearly, Butler's return had long-term expectations.

However, an unexpected opportunity to stake a permanent claim to the full-back position then opened quite unexpectedly for Pat. Following a serious leg injury sustained in the 1946 All-Ireland final, Mick Butler was unable to take part in any of Kilkenny's opening 1946/47 National League games. The selectors turned to Pat and whether his selection was intended to be short-term only made no impact on him as he grabbed his opportunity with both hands.

He made his debut in Kilkenny's opening National League game against Waterford in October, and held down his place for the remaining pre-winter break games. When Mick Butler, still living and playing his club hurling in Dublin, subsequently declined to declare for Kilkenny for the 1947 season, Pat became the county's first-choice full-back. Thus his senior inter-county career was effectively launched at an age when most players might have considered that such an opportunity had passed them by.

Another development occurred early in 1947 that significantly benefited the progression of Pat's regenerated career. In the absence of a strict Parish Rule high-profile junior club players were consistently seduced by the more successful senior clubs to transfer to them, a temptation few of them resisted. Thus, when the 1947 county Championship began, Pat was wearing the full-back jersey of Eire Og, the champions of 1944 and 1945, and short odds to take the 1947 title. He was now immersed at the highest level at both club and county.

Pat won his first senior provincial medal in July, 1947, when Kilkenny easily defeated Dublin by a 16-point margin in the final. Curiously, Dublin's full-back in that game was Dunamaggin's Davey Walsh, whose brothers, Tom and Jim 'Link', would themselves subsequently enjoy very successful Kilkenny inter-county careers. In the All-Ireland semi-final Kilkenny had a one-point win over Railway Cup winners, Galway, courtesy of two late points from Jim Langton and Terry Leahy. All match reports noted the outstanding display given by Pat on the edge of the Kilkenny square.

There was extreme internal pressure heaped on Kilkenny as they prepared to challenge Cork in the final. The county's last All-Ireland success in 1939 was followed by the drought in the early years of the new decade, where only a single provincial title was won, and more recently by the All-Ireland final defeats of 1945 and 1946 by Tipperary and Cork, respectively. A third successive All-Ireland final defeat in as many years was unthinkable.

Kilkenny entered the game as clear outsiders, their chances reflected in the attendance of only 61,510 – almost 8,000 down on the 1945 final, and 4,000 down on the 1946 final. By the end of a breathtaking game Kilkenny emerged winners by a one-point margin. That final is generally regarded as one of the greatest ever, from the aspect of the sheer quality of the hurling played, the tough but disciplined man-to-man exchanges, the several outstanding individual performances, the almost suffocating tension throughout, and the dramatic late winning score. That was the ultimate game.

—m—

Pat was undoubtedly one of Kilkenny's most influential players that historic day. In its match report, *The Kilkenny People* noted that, "Pat Hayden was if anything better than against Galway, and saying that is certainly paying him a huge tribute." Having played magnificently in the opening half, Pat was switched to the unfamiliar centre-back position after half time to replace the injured Peter Prendergast with Championship debutant, Tullaroan's Ned Kavanagh, slotting into the full-back position. Despite his new surroundings, and charged with the daunting task of marking Christy Ring, Pat continued to perform magnificently, holding Cork's main attacker scoreless from play for the remainder of the game. Terry Leahy's late winning point gave Kilkenny the long overdue 13th title and etched Pat's name in the directory of Kilkenny's All -Ireland winning full backs.

Having broken its losing sequence Kilkenny were expected to develop as a team and to at least retain their titles. Whether through complacency, faulty preparation or poor selection policy, the team did not progress as it should have. They lost the delayed replay of the 1946-47 National League final to Limerick (played in March, 1948), and, two months later, were sensationally defeated by Laois in the Leinster semi-final. The following year, 1949, was equally unproductive as Laois again proved their masters, this time in the Leinster final played at Nowlan Park.

The first year of the new decade saw an improvement in Kilkenny's fortunes. A defeat by Tipperary in the National League final was a set-back but at least the team was becoming competitive again. They regained the Leinster title with a narrow win over a resurgent Nicky Rackard-led Wexford at a packed Nowlan Park. However, in the space of a few months, Kilkenny narrowly lost a second national final to Tipperary, this time the All-Ireland. That defeat is one all Kilkenny followers, and most neutrals who were present, feel that Kilkenny should have won. Despite having played against a stiff breeze in the first half, Kilkenny led by two points at half time. However, wayward shooting from play, frees, 70s, and sideline cuts by a succession of hitherto accurate forwards, left the door ajar for Tipperary to slink through by a single point in a low-scoring game, 1-9 to 1-8.

That avoidable defeat seriously dented the team's confidence and, by extension, its progression. An ideal opportunity to banish the painful memories of the defeats of 1948 and 1949 had been spurned. Instead, Kilkenny dipped deeper into a period of decline, winning only a solitary provincial title, in 1953, over the following six Championships.

Their main challengers in Leinster all benefited from Kilkenny's travails. Laois remained competitive, as Kilkenny would discover again to their cost in the 1951 Leinster semi-final. Dublin had assembled a formidable team and would contest two Leinster finals, 1952 and 1954, winning the former. However, the foremost obstacle to a Kilkenny resurgence came from a new source, Wexford. Though out of the limelight for almost 40 years, Wexford had demonstrated signs of a renaissance in the mid-1940s. Yet few within the hurling fraternity could have envisaged the dominant force Wexford would become by the mid-1950s

Wexford's progressive climb to hurling's summit was flagged in their laudable effort against Kilkenny at Nowlan Park in that 1950 Leinster final, falling short only by a goal. They won the Leinster Championship in 1951, defeating Kilkenny's conquerors Laois, in the final. Inexperience, and an unaddressed goalkeeping problem, derailed their All-Ireland title ambitions against Tipperary in that year's final. That Wexford still proved too strong for Kilkenny in the 1952 Leinster semi-final without the services of their injured spiritual leader, Nicky Rackard, was a firm statement that their recent resurgence was no mere transitory phenomenon.

In 1953, Kilkenny regrouped and regained the provincial title to give Pat his third and last Leinster medal. That Championship run came to a disappointing end in the All-Ireland semi-final, as, in a repeat of the wastefulness that cost them the 1950 All-Ireland title, Kilkenny allowed Galway to progress to the final by a single point.

Matters were about to get considerably worse for Pat, and Kilkenny. In the 1954 Leinster semi-final Kilkenny incurred its most comprehensive provincial Championship defeat since 1896, when Wexford dished out a 5-11 to 0-7 drubbing. Pat's first-half injury and subsequent withdrawal could not be aired as the sole cause of Kilkenny's collapse. It was evident to all within the county that a new team had to be created, but, as Wexford were getting stronger and more difficult to keep pace with, time was not on Pat's side.

Unlike some of his long-term comrades, such as Jim Langton, Ramie Dowling and Dan Kennedy, Pat did not retire following that Wexford debacle. Due to persistent knee problems he did not feature in any of Kilkenny's 1954-55 National League games, and was not a panellist in Kilkenny's wins in the 1955 Leinster quarter- and semi-final wins. He was, however, added to the panel for the final against Wexford but did not see any action in either the draw or replay, which Kilkenny lost. His name did not again appear on a Kilkenny team list. He was then in his 40th year.

Incidentally, for that 1955 Championship, and again in 1956, which also ended in Leinster final defeat by Wexford, Kilkenny were forced to play stylish corner-back John Maher at full-back, a position which suited neither his physique nor his hurling ability. The search for Pat's replacement would go on.

Though Wexford had become Kilkenny's nemesis during the latter part of Pat's career, he personally benefited from their regular battles in terms of his own reputation as a hurling character. Over those years Pat had formed a unique friendship with Wexford's iconic leader, and one of the country's best known sportsmen, Nicky Rackard. Despite being in direct opposition in numerous tense League and Championship games for almost a decade, both men became extremely close friends. That both enjoyed post-match drinks together only added to the mystique of their relationship. In none of their many clashes did either man take any advantage over the other by rough-house tactics. The media and the hurling public were fully aware of the players' friendship and much capital was generated by it. Being regular colleagues on Leinster Railway Cup teams for almost that decade further cemented their relationship. Though six years older than his great friend, Pat was amongst the legions of hurling followers who attended the legendary Rathnure man's funeral in April, 1976, following his untimely death, some few days short of his 54th birthday.

Pat earned inter-provincial selection after only a year of senior inter-county hurling. Having established himself as one of the county's most accomplished full-backs during that successful 1947 Championship, he was selected on Leinster's 1948 Railway Cup team. For the remaining years of his career he was his province's first-choice full-back. On St Patrick's Day 1954, an attendance of 49,023 saw Pat win his only Railway Cup medal as Leinster broke a losing sequence in finals that stretched back to 1942 He was then a few days short of his 38th birthday. Pat played in the losing finals of 1948, 1950, 1951 and 1953.

Like the Railway Cup, the Oireachtas Tournament was a highly regarded competition during Pat's career. In 1947, he won his only Oireachtas medal, which, incidentally, was the year that the organisers decided that the tournament would be exclusively for hurling and for which the winners would receive An Corn Thomais Aghas. Pat also played in the losing 1951 final.

Though Pat played in two National League finals, 1947 (replayed in 1948) and 1954 and a 'Home' final in 1950, he ended his career without a National League title. That 1954 final defeat was a forerunner of things to come that summer as Tipperary handed out a 3-10 to 1-4 thrashing. Perhaps the subsequent mauling by Wexford in the Leinster semi-final was not the major shock that the hurling world perceived it to be.

Kilkenny did not undertake any American tours during Pat's time with the team. The closest he came to winning such a trip was in 1950 but Kilkenny's 'Home' final defeat by Tipperary saw the Munstermen earn the trip to New York where they defeated the locals in the final proper. Pat did make several trips to London for the annual Whit Festival where Kilkenny were frequently invited to compete for the prestigious Monaghan Cup. In 1948, he gave an outstanding display in Kilkenny's 5-8 to 3-4 win over Tipperary, played before an attendance of over 23,000 at Mitcham Stadium.

At club level, Pat won his sole senior Championship title in 1947, in Eire Og's 3-10 to 0-13 over Tullaroan. Two features around that game are worth noting. Firstly it took place a mere two weeks prior to the Kilkenny-Cork All-Ireland final, in which 13 of the Kilkenny panel were involved, an occurrence which would simply not be entertained nowadays. Secondly, Tullaroan's Ned Kavanagh, a player who had never previously featured on a Kilkenny panel played so well in that county final that he was added to the Kilkenny panel some days prior to the final, taking part in only a very limited number of training sessions. Kavanagh was subsequently introduced as a second-half substitute, playing the remaining 25 minutes at full-back, with Pat switching successfully to centre-back. As his personal situation decreed, those 25 minutes were the full extent of Kavanagh's All-Ireland medal-winning inter-county career. He was ordained to the priesthood in June, 1948, and never resumed his Kilkenny career, spending all the years since then ministering in California where he still resides.

Pat later played in the 1950 county final but Eire Og, despite having an array of other high-profile players such as Ramie Dowling, Tommy Murphy, Eddie Carew (Waterford and Munster), Jim Langton, Liam Reidy, Paddy O'Brien and Padraig Lennon, were defeated by Dicksboro, following a replay.

Pat 'Diamond' Hayden's senior inter-county career was unique in many respects. It began at an age when most players of a similar age would be considering retirement. He won a Railway Cup medal some days short of his 38th birthday and was on a Leinster final panel while in his 40th year. Clearly longevity was not an issue that unduly troubled him. Though not a big man, standing at 5' 9", and weighing around 12 stone, he successfully pitted his hurling skills and his legendary wits against some of the greatest full-forwards the game has known. He played in a position where no questions were asked, but was never known to have resorted to unsporting tactics against an opponent. He became one of the game's real characters but in so doing he never lost sight of what his primary duties were. He enjoyed the fanfare and the publicity surrounding his duels and his friendship with Nicky Rackard, but was never distracted by them.

Pat began his working life at Hennessy's, Barracore, Goresbridge. He was primarily a lorry driver throughout his working life. He spent a brief time in England in the early 1950s and also worked at Mount Juliet Estate in

Thomastown, where he played cricket and tennis to a high standard. Following his marriage to Maureen Cody, Pat moved to Callan where Maureen ran the well-known Cody's Shop and Restaurant. Pat died on January 16, 1979, with Maureen later passing away on September 14, 1981. The Haydens are survived by their only child, Martin, the prominent senior counsel, who resides in Dublin.

I have many treasured memories from my association with sport and sporting events. One involves Pat and relates back to Nowlan Park on Sunday, April 27, 1969. My club, The Rower-Inistioge were getting ready to face the might of Bennettsbridge in the delayed 1968 county senior final. As the second youngest of an inexperienced team playing in its first senior final, needless to say, the nerves were somewhat stretched. Shortly before we left the dressing room a burly figure in a white raincoat entered and, having sought permission from club officials, gave the team a brief talk and wished us the best of luck. It was none other than Pat, wielding his own brand of magic, one which was probably not the main reason why we won, but was in itself a memorable start to what became a memorable day.

Numerous theories abound as to the origins of Pat's nickname, 'The Diamond'. Probably the most plausible is that despite his light-hearted disposition Pat was a doughty, durable character when necessary, and consequently was compared to a diamond, one of the world's hardest materials. Once the comparison was made, it fastened tightly.

Tom Williams, in his excellent biography of Nicky Rackard, entitled Cuchulainn's Son, quotes his subject's opinion of all the great players he encountered during his lengthy career. In relation to Pat, Rackard had this to say: "I have met some good full-backs, tough full-backs and friendly full-backs, but in all my years I have met only one 'Diamond' Hayden. For about eight years 'Diamond' and I used to clash regularly. I always enjoyed playing on the brave 'Diamond' for he was a great piece of stuff. He was no parlour hurler but he never did me a mean stroke." A fitting tribute to one of the best from one of the best.

CAREER HIGHLIGHTS

All-Ireland senior finalist: 1947 and 1950

All-Ireland senior winner: 1947

Leinster senior winner: 1947, 1950 and 1953

Railway Cup winner: 1954

All-Ireland junior winner: 1946

Leinster junior winner: 1946

Oireachtas Tournament winner: 1947

County senior winner: 1947

Monaghan Cup winner: 1948

National League finalist: 1947, 1950 (home final) and 1954.

ALL-IRELAND WINNING TEAMS

1947
September 7
Kilkenny 0-14 Cork 2-7
Croke Park
Attendance 61,510

Kilkenny: Jim Donegan (Eoghan Ruadh, Dublin), Paddy Grace (Dicksboro), Pat 'Diamond' Hayden (Eire Og), Mark Marnell (Tullaroan), Jimmy Kelly (Carrickshock), Peter Prendergast (Thomastown), Jack Mulcahy (Eire Og), Dan Kennedy, captain (Thomastown), Jimmy Heffernan (Carrickshock), Tom Walton (Tullaroan), Terry Leahy (Faughs, Dublin), Jim Langton (Eire Og), Shem Downey (Tullaroan), Bill Cahill (Graigue), Liam Reidy (Eire Og).

Subs: Paddy 'Chunky' O'Brien (Eire Og), Nick O'Donnell (Eire Og), Padraigh Lennon (Eire Og), Tommy Murphy (Eire Og), Jack Egan (Tullaroan), Ned Kavanagh (Tullaroan), replaced Prendergast (injured, 35 mins), Bill Walsh (Carrickshock).

Walsh was selected to play at left corner-back but was withdrawn prior to the game due to injury and was replaced by Jimmy Heffernan. Mark Marnell moved from left half-back to replace Walsh, with Jack Mulcahy moving from midfield to left half-back to replace Marnell. Heffernan replaced Mulcahy at midfield.

Walsh

Jim 'Link' Walsh (left of main photo in a 1962 Walsh Cup game) manned the centre of the full-back line as Kilkenny ended a 10-year gap by winning a 14th All-Ireland title in an unforgettable struggle with Waterford.
Walsh is also pictured on the left of back row in the photo of the Leinster 1963 Railway Cup team, and (bottom) action from the drawn 1959 All-Ireland final.

chapter 6

As the 1956 hurling year was drawing to a close, Kilkenny would, at best, have been awarded no higher than fourth place in a shortlist of likely winners of the 1957 Championship. Tipperary and Cork, with three titles each, and Wexford with two, had won the eight most recent All-Ireland finals. Even a Leinster title win looked beyond Kilkenny's capabilities at that point. In addition to these two All-Ireland titles, Wexford were also National League, Oireachtas Tournament and Walsh Cup title holders, and, perhaps more dauntingly, were seeking a unique four-in-a-row Leinster titles. Kilkenny followers of even the most optimistic nature saw little prospect of the Wexford bandwagon being derailed by their team in the immediate future.

By 1956, Wexford's hurling renaissance, first noted in the mid-1940s, had acquired an air of permanency, while Kilkenny's recent decline showed no immediate signs of abating. That decline was difficult to understand. Kilkenny had won the Leinster Championship in 1953, had qualified for the 1954 National League final, and had supplied nine players to the Leinster team that won the 1954 Railway Cup title with a memorable win over a formidable Tipperary-Cork influenced Munster side. Yet, within a few months, with all their Leinster men on duty Kilkenny were totally outclassed by Wexford in the Leinster semi-final by 5-11 to 0-7 – the county's heaviest provincial Championship defeat that century. While Kilkenny ran Wexford close in the provincial finals of 1955 and 1956, the harsh reality was that the only trophy won during those years was the 1955 Walsh Cup, played in April, 1956, with a 2-10 to 3-6 defeat of Westmeath. That only three Kilkenny players made the successful 1956 Leinster team, as against Wexford's nine, was in itself an indication of where the power base of Leinster hurling then lay.

Clearly part of the cause of Kilkenny's inability to remain seriously competitive was the failure to find adequate replacements for the number of high-profile players from the 1947-1955 era, who had retired. Amongst the positions that were causing concern was that of full-back. That Pat 'Diamond' Hayden was recalled to the panel for the 1955 Leinster final, though by then in his 40th year, demonstrates the plight of the selectors in finding his replacement. For that year's Championship, and that of 1956, Kilkenny were forced to play stylish John Maher at full-back, a position for which he was totally unsuited, despite his all-round hurling skills. With the arrival on the scene like a force of nature of Ollie Walsh in 1956, it was essential, if Kilkenny were to profit from his many talents, and help him propel them to a return to the limelight, that a custom-made full-back with long-term prospects be found.

—◊—

Sport, like life itself, rarely remains static for long. Unknown to the wider hurling audience, Kilkenny's full-back predicament was actually in the course of resolving itself during 1956. In late September, Kilkenny were waiting to play the All-Ireland junior final with a burly 23-year-old farmer, Jim 'Link' Walsh, manning the full-back position. Such was the impact he made in Kilkenny's progress to that final that he was promoted to the senior team for an Oireachtas Tournament semi-final game against Galway. His display in that game, and later in the Junior final win, ensured his selection for the Oireachtas Tournament and Walsh Cup finals that soon followed. Jim was subsequently ever-present during all of Kilkenny's pre-Christmas National League games, his impressive displays throughout giving followers a genuine feeling of optimism that Kilkenny had eventually found a replacement for 'The Diamond', a replacement around which a strong defensive unit could be built and one that would enable Ollie Walsh to demonstrate his spell-binding array of skills. Jim 'Link' Walsh's career was now on the national stage, a career which would be marked with some memorable moments, a few heartbreaks, but also one that was characterised by the sheer honesty with which it was played out.

Jim Link Walsh was born on April 15, 1933 to John and Anastatia Walsh (formerly Heneberry), a farming family from Ballintee, Dunamaggin. Jim had three brothers, Davey, Pat and Tom, and one sister, Alice. His early education at the local national school and later at Callan CBS was interspersed with as much hurling as was permissible. Like the majority of their neighbours, the Walsh family was a 'hurling family' where, once work commitments were attended to, hurling took precedence to all other pursuits. All of Jim's brothers played the game, with both Davey and Tom becoming particularly prominent. Davey subsequently played with Dublin at full-back in their defeat by Waterford in the 1948 All-Ireland final.

Davey later played with Waterford and Munster, winning two Railway Cup medals with his adopted province. He also won Waterford senior and intermediate championships with Tourin. Tom, who was three years older than Jim, won both a senior county title with Carrickshock and an All-Ireland junior title with Kilkenny in 1951. Later on, his career ran side by side with that of Jim's, the brothers sharing in many memorable Kilkenny wins throughout the 1950s and early 1960s.

Jim's early promise as a hurler of rich potential was rewarded in 1950 when he won a county minor title with Eoghan Ruadh (Callan) and Leinster and All-Ireland minor medals with Kilkenny. A second Leinster title followed in 1951, but a defeat by Galway in the semi-final thwarted further All-Ireland ambitions.

The introduction of the Parish Rule in 1954 initiated a positive dynamic to club hurling within the county. Its introduction gave a fresh impetus to the development of the parish team, fulfilling one of the original objectives of the Association's founding fathers. Players could now only play for their parish team, or wherever they were officially resident after being properly transferred. In compliance with the new order, Jim and Tom transferred back to Dunamaggin, their southern-based parish team, then playing at junior level.

It is a tribute to both players that, despite not having experienced any notable club successes with Dunamaggin, they both earned selection on the county junior team in 1956, ending the year as All-Ireland winners. That team was a particularly formidable outfit, scoring an impressive 33 goals and 42 points while conceding a miserly 11 goals and 30 points in their five games. It is worth noting that the team was able to endure the loss of Ollie Walsh, Billie Dwyer and Paddy Hoban through promotion to the senior team, but were still able to win the All-Ireland title.

—〜〜—

As already noted, following that junior success Jim saw out the end of 1956 as Kilkenny first choice full-back. His reputation as player of serious potential was cemented when, in March, 1957, despite not having yet played a senior inter-county Championship game, he was selected as full-back on The Rest of Ireland team that faced an Ireland Selection at Croke Park in a representative game. An attendance of over 20,000 saw Jim renew his rivalry with Nicky Rackard, first formed in those Oireachtas Tournament and Walsh Cup finals of the previous autumn, holding the great man scoreless from play. That Jim was able to perform so effectively and maturely against an attack, which, in addition to Rackard, included such household names as Tim Flood, Ned Wheeler, Sean Clohessy, Paddy Kenny and Christy Ring, spoke eloquently as to his progress in the top grade.

By April Jim was back in Croke Park for the National League final. Though Kilkenny lost to Tipperary, Jim was now acquiring the valuable Croke Park experience that would profit him enormously as his career developed. Despite that defeat, Kilkenny looked more settled than for some time, with the full-back line, which Jim shared with brother Tom and John Maher, looking the ideal barrier to front Ollie Walsh. The outlook for Kilkenny's Championship prospects were no longer as bleak as many pundits had earlier predicted.

Having disposed of Dublin after a replay, Kilkenny now faced Wexford in the Leinster final. Those Dublin games heralded the initial instalments of the soon-to-be legendary duels between Jim and Dublin's robust full-forward, Tony Young. A player with strong Tullaroan connections, Young was a difficult opponent, one element of whose game was to see how frequently he could dispatch the opposition goalkeeper into his own net – with or without the ball. That Jim had other ideas, particularly in relation to the well-being of Ollie Walsh, guaranteed that some memorable afternoons ensued between the two big men.

That 1957 Leinster final generated unprecedented interest countrywide. Wexford's overall popularity and the uniqueness of their quest for a fourth successive provincial title brought a record Leinster final attendance of 52,272 to Croke Park. Wexford began the game as if determined to choke the life out Kilkenny as early as possible before a serious challenge could be mounted. Through the brilliance of Ollie Walsh and the defiance of his full back line, Wexford's outfield superiority was not reflected on the scoreboard. By the second quarter Kilkenny had settled into the game to such an extent that, between then and half-time, the issue was settled. A five-goal scoring blitz gave Kilkenny an interval lead of 5-5 to Wexford's 1-3. At the end of one of the most memorable hour's hurling in Kilkenny's history, the Leinster title was regained by a margin of 16 points (6-9 to 1-5).

Once again, Jim had negated the threat of Nicky Rackard, conceding neither scores nor frees to Wexford's main scoring medium. That the 'father figure' of Wexford's hurling resurgence was shortly to surrender to the ravages of over 16 years at the pinnacle in both codes, and to a career-long knee injury, should not in any respect detract from the magnitude of Jim's achievement.

By September, Kilkenny had won their 14th All-Ireland title following an unforgettable struggle with Waterford, one that was only decided by a last-minute point. That final was the first in a trilogy of Kilkenny-Waterford finals of that era, all games being noteworthy for their free-flowing hurling, dramatic finishes, memorable individual performances and periods of mesmerising attacking play. At that game's end, Kilkenny had bridged that ten-year gap without an All-Ireland success, and Jim had become the county's sixth All-Ireland winning full-back.

Jim, by year's end, had cemented his reputation as no-frills, highly dependable, fundamentalist-style full-back. His approach to the position differed to that of his contemporaries such as Nick O'Donnell, Noel

Drumgoole or Austin Flynn. Those players mixed the close exchanges, which characterised full-back play, with high catches and long clearances. Jim, on the other hand, limited his duties to providing Ollie Walsh with as much cover as was possible, and permissible, in the belief that such an approach best suited the situation. Over time, he developed a style of play that was marked with an excellent positional sense, employing deft flicks and neat touches out of the danger area. There was many a full-forward who was forced, in the course of a game, to re-assess his pre-match appraisal of Jim's hurling ability.

The 1957 success was Jim's sole senior All-Ireland win. Further opportunities arose in 1958 and 1959, but, on each occasion, Kilkenny came up short. The 1958 defeat to Tipperary in the All-Ireland semi-final was disappointing, as, only a point in arrears at the break, Kilkenny surrendered their title following a very subdued second-half performance. In 1959, Kilkenny lost the final to Waterford after a replay. The real heartbreak for Jim was not so much the eventual defeat but the manner by which Waterford snatched the draw. Kilkenny appeared to have the game won as they defended a three-point lead with the clock ticking towards full time. Waterford's Seamus Power, in a brave attempt to salvage the game, fired a hard shot from close range towards the Kilkenny goal. Ollie Walsh appeared to have the shot covered, but Jim, in his own attempt to block the ball, managed only to divert it off his own hurley and into the net for the equaliser.

Paddy Buggy, Kilkenny's wing back that day, and later President of the Association, recently remarked: "Such was Jim's standing within the panel and with Kilkenny followers that not once did I hear any criticism of his misfortunate attempt to save Seamus Power's equalising shot." Waterford won the replay by a comfortable eight points.

Jim's year came to a relatively satisfactory conclusion with a second Oireachtas Tournament title. That final win over Galway was notable for two reasons. Firstly, it came courtesy of a late rally that saw them recover from an 11-point deficit midway through the second half, to win by two points (6-6 to 5-8). Secondly, that rally was instigated by the switch of Ollie Walsh from goal, where he was in difficulty all day, to the forward line. Shortly after his switch Ollie scored a brilliant goal to set off the recovery.

Injury and illness respectively, prevented Jim from playing in Kilkenny's

Leinster Championship defeats by Wexford in 1960 and 1961. He returned for the 1961-62 National League, which Kilkenny won, defeating a Christy Ring-led Cork in the final. Following that win, Kilkenny were installed as favourites to win the All-Ireland, but a generally poor performance in the Leinster final against Wexford put an end to their aspirations. A particularly lacklustre first-half display saw Kilkenny enter the break seven points in arrears (3-5 to 1-4), and despite an improved second-half they never really looked likely winners. Jim, and Seamus Cleere and Billy Dwyer, were Kilkenny's best players on a very forgettable day.

Jim's closing Championship commitments were brief. Playing against Wexford in the 1963 Leinster semi-final he encountered difficulties with the pace of the game and was replaced at half-time. Though on the panel for the Leinster final win over Dublin, he later withdrew, accepting that, through work obligations, he could no longer train or play to the required standard.

Jim played in New York's Gaelic Park during Kilkenny's American tour in 1958. That year he also played at London's Wembley Stadium on the occasion of the first staging of the Whit Weekend Wembley Gaelic Games Festival organised by the London GAA Board. These games were major cultural and sporting events for the Irish community in Britain, attracting attendances in excess of 40,000 to the home of British football.

Prior to the establishment of those games, county teams travelled annually to London to battle for the coveted Monaghan Cup. In 1957, Kilkenny, with the nucleus of the team that would win that year's All-Ireland title, defeated Tipperary on a 3-6 to 1-5 scoreline, to take the trophy for the first time that decade in a game played at Woolwich. The following year, as noted, the tournament, with the Monaghan Cup still on offer, moved to Wembley Stadium where it remained until falling attendances caused its cancellation in 1975. Kilkenny, with their full All-Ireland winning team on board, were the inaugural winners of that 1958 Wembley Stadium experiment by defeating Clare.

Despite his almost telepathic understanding with Leinster's regular goalkeeper, Ollie Walsh, Jim was largely ignored by the provinces selectors. He did make the panel in 1959 but Connacht defeated Leinster in the semi-final. Curiously, Jim did make the team in 1963, a few short months prior to his retirement. He was extremely unlucky not to have then added a Railway

Cup medal to his collection as Leinster were defeated in the replayed final by a point, the first inter-provincial final to require a replay.

Jim did not experience much success at club level. He did play in two South junior finals, 1958 and 1966, winning the latter year but subsequently losing the county final to Galmoy. Jim did, however, play senior Championship hurling for one year. In 1961 the County Board, in an attempt to reinvigorate a somewhat stagnant senior Championship, allowed four divisional teams, comprised of players from junior clubs, to participate in the Championship. Jim's team, the Near South, reached the county final, but despite having an array of other county players on board, were unable to prevent a Pa Dillon-inspired St Lachtain's from taking the title. The experiment was not repeated.

For the purposes of this project I experienced the pleasure of meeting Jim's brother, Tom, at his home in Callan. Tom regaled me with illuminating tales about both their careers – the memorable wins, the heartbreaking defeats, and the great friends they both made from their hurling exploits. Tom wistfully recalled the few 'incidents', some wholesome, others not so, that occurred during their guardianship of the Kilkenny square. He stressed that, rather than those 'incidents' hindering the creation of friendships between the players involved, they only served to cement them. "We all accepted the unwritten rule that, once the game was over, what may have or may have not happened on the field was never carried over afterwards. Once the final whistle blew, that was it. Any lingering hostilities were between the supporters rather than the players," remarked Tom.

Tom took the opportunity to dispel a modern-day view that players of his and Jim's era, and indeed, players of earlier days, had a somewhat relaxed attitude towards physical fitness and team preparation. "Jim and I spent many hours training and practising during the off-season on the farm," he recalled, "and I have no doubt that the majority of our contemporaries prepared likewise. It would not have been possible for us to have played in so many memorable games against so many great players if we were not properly prepared". He is unable, however, to shed any light on the origins of Jim's nickname. "He always had it," noted Tom.

—ᐉᐁ—

During his career Jim pitted his wits, his individualistic style, and his strength against some of hurling's most celebrated full-forwards. Players such as Christy Ring, Nicky Rackard, Tom Ryan, Johnny Kiely, Tony Young, Donal Whelan and other household names, all consistently challenged Jim, but none mastered him. He was extremely popular with Kilkenny followers who appreciated his honest, wholehearted approach. His well-established personal friendship with the charismatic Ollie Walsh only added to his own appeal.

When asked in an interview in 1957 as to who was the best full-back then playing, Ollie Walsh replied: "They are all good, but give me 'The Link' any time." Surely the ultimate accolade.

Jim 'Link' Walsh died in July, 1994. He never married.

CAREER HIGHLIGHTS

All-Ireland senior finalist: 1957 and 1959 (Replay)

All-Ireland senior winner: 1957

Leinster senior winner: 1957, 1958, 1959 and1963 (s)

All-Ireland junior winner: 1956

Leinster junior winner: 1956

All-Ireland minor winner: 1950

Leinster minor winner: 1950 and 1951

Oireachtas tournament winner: 1957 and 1959

National League winner: 1961/62

Walsh Cup winner: 1957, 1958 1959 and 1962

Railway Cup finalist: 1963

County minor winner: 1950

South Kilkenny winner: 1966

Rest of Ireland selection: 1957

Monaghan Cup Winner:1957

Wembley Tournament winner: 1958

American tour: 1958

ALL-IRELAND WINNING TEAMS

1957
September 1
Kilkenny 4-10 Waterford 3-12
Croke Park
Attendance 70,594

Kilkenny: Ollie Walsh (Thomastown), Tom Walsh (Dunamaggin), Jim 'Link' Walsh (Dunamaggin), John Maher (Crokes, Dublin), Paddy Buggy (Slieverue), Mickey Walsh (Slieverue), Johnny McGovern (Bennettsbridge), John Sutton (Mullinavat), Mick Brophy (Danesfort), Denis Heaslip (Knocktopher), Mick Kenny (John Lockes), Mickey Kelly, captain (Bennettsbridge), Dick Rockett (Slieverue), Billy Dwyer (Foulkstown), Sean Clohosey (Young Irelands, Dublin).

Subs: Ned Fenlon (St Vincent's, Graiguenamanagh), Jimmy Murphy (Carrickshock), PJ Garvan (Dicksboro), Bill Walsh (Young Irelands, Dublin) replaced John Sutton (injured, 48 mins), Liam Cleere (Bennettsbridge), Jim Hogan (Moindearg, Dublin).

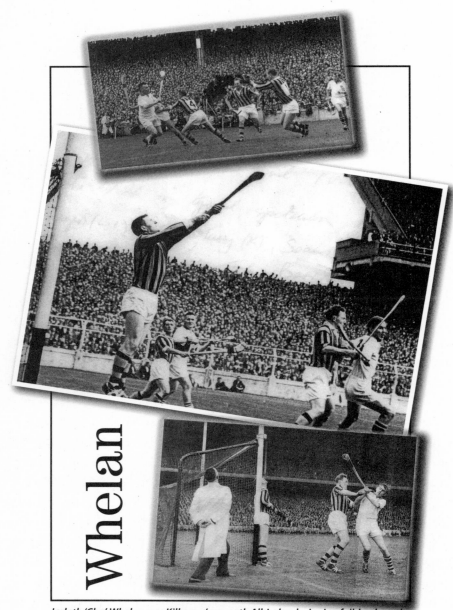

Whelan

Jarlath 'Cha' Whelan was Kilkenny's seventh All-Ireland winning full-back, and his Championship career in the No.3 shirt was, by far, the briefest. It began on Sunday, July 5, 1963, and had run its course by All-Ireland Sunday, but Whelan also found fame on hurling fields in Dublin and London.

chapter 7

Of Kilkenny's 14 All-Ireland winning full-backs, the Championship career of Jarlath 'Cha' Whelan was, by far, the briefest. It began on Sunday, July 5, 1963, and had run its course on All-Ireland Sunday, some seven weeks later. While Cha, as he was universally known, did figure in both corner-back positions in Championship and non-Championship games regularly over the following four years, he did not again regain the full-back berth, then almost exclusively filled by Pa Dillon, except for one year by Jimmy Lynch.

Yet, for all its brevity, Cha's career as the county's Championship full-back covered important Leinster and All-Ireland wins, the former being Kilkenny's first since 1959, the latter bridging a gap that stretched back to 1957. Both of those wins were crucially timed in the progression of Kilkenny hurling, with Cha playing his part.

Cha was born on September 7, 1939, to John and Joan Whelan of Oldtown, Thomastown. He attended Stoneyford National School, which, though not in the parish of Thomastown, was the school nearest to the family home at Oldtown. He played schools' hurling while there but without any notable successes. At Under-16 and minor level Cha played with the Thomastown parish team

When Cha was in his late teenage years there were two adult clubs in the parish, Thomastown and Thomastown Rangers. The Rangers drew most of their players and supporters from the southern and western sides of the parish, which included the Oldtown area, so, naturally, Cha signed up with them. In 1961, however, work commitments found him in Dublin where he joined Faughs, one of the city's most celebrated clubs. As team-mates in his new surroundings Cha had two former Kilkenny All-Ireland hurlers, Billie Dwyer and Paddy Kelly. Curiously, his only club championship outing with his new club was a losing one, to Moindearg, a club which drew its players exclusively from Dublin-based Kilkenny natives.

Cha's consistently impressive Dublin league performances with Faughs gradually filtered down to Kilkenny, earning him selection for Kilkenny's two remaining 1960-61 National League games against Dublin and Waterford, playing at full-back.

Facing into the 1961 Championship Kilkenny had an unsettled team, with almost half of the positions undecided. In an attempt by the selectors to monitor all the available talent, a series of trial games were held under the guise of The Vincent De Paul Tournament, the participating teams being The Near South, The Far South, The City, and The North. A Kilkenny Exiles' Selection was chosen to play the winners. Cha played right corner-back for the Exiles, their full-back position going to Tony Bennett, formerly from Bennetsbridge, but then playing with Moindearg. Curiously when Jim 'Link' Walsh (Near South), the regular Kilkenny full-back, subsequently withdrew from the county panel due to injury; none of the other full-backs used in the tournament, Tom Nolan (Far South), Jim Hennessy (The City), Pa Dillon (The North) or Tony Bennett were selected for the Leinster semi-final against Wexford – the full-back position going to Tullaroan's Jim Hennessy who had played corner-back on The North team. Cha did not make the 1961 Championship panel.

By the end of 1961, Cha found himself in London where he joined the Sean McDermott's club with whom he won a London senior Championship title in 1962. He was back in Ireland that September playing full-back for London in their unsuccessful Intermediate All-Ireland final clash with Carlow. Returning home permanently later that year Cha joined Thomastown, who had just recently won the county junior Championship and would be playing in the senior grade in 1963.

Though then playing senior club hurling, Cha was eligible for that year's Kilkenny intermediate team. However, having played impressively for the senior team in a tournament game against Waterford, the intermediate selectors decided not to play him in their opening Championship game, leaving him at the disposal of the senior selectors. When the team to play Wexford in the Leinster semi-final was announced Cha was selected at right corner-back.

Arriving at Croke Park for the game Cha felt unwell and withdrew from the starting team, being replaced by Fan Larkin. At half time the selectors, concerned with the uncertainty in the full-back line withdrew full-back Jim 'Link' Walsh, sending in Cha as a direct replacement. That Wexford only scored one goal and one point in the second half illustrates the immediate impact which Cha had on proceedings. His mastery of the previously influential Ned Wheeler was deemed a significant contributor to Kilkenny's hard-fought four-point win.

Following Kilkenny's comfortable win over Dublin in the Leinster final, Cha found himself preparing for an All-Ireland final with only 90 minutes of senior Championship experience behind him. On his display against Dublin, The Kilkenny People noted: "Cha Whelan did a good job in protecting Ollie Walsh and also held Paddy Croke scoreless, not a simple feat in his first Leinster final."

Kilkenny's opponents in the All-Ireland final were Waterford, who were clear favourites following recent impressive wins over Tipperary in the National League and Munster finals The game became a high-scoring thriller, where both defences leaked scores incessantly. The scoring deluge, loose play, and the frantic finish made the game very entertaining for the 73,125 patrons, an attendance that was not bettered until the 2002 final. In all the mayhem that took place around both goalmouths, Cha had the distinction of keeping his direct opponent, John Barron, scoreless. In the end Kilkenny survived by a three-point margin, giving Cha seventh place in the exclusive ranks of Kilkenny All-Ireland winning full-backs.

Cha was back in Croke Park the following Sunday, where he won his third senior medal in Kilkenny's four-point win over Wexford in the Walsh Cup final, then a highly regarded competition.

The final act of Cha's tenure as Kilkenny's regular full-back was now imminent. That took place at Nowlan Park in late September when Tipperary arrived for an Oireachtas Tournament semi-final. They were clearly determined to dent the reputation of the new champions, and to prove that their own recent big-game defeats by Waterford were no more than sporting aberrations. Tipperary ran Kilkenny ragged in the opening half, the local full-back line creaking under the relentless pressure. Changes were made at half-time, the major one being the introduction of Pa Dillon to full-back, with Cha moving to right-corner.

For the remainder of the 1963 season, and the early months of 1964, Cha was consistently selected for Kilkenny's National League and tournament games, usually at right corner-back. Kilkenny's failure to qualify for the knockout stages of the League denied them valuable competitive pre-Championship games. However, as All-Ireland champions, Kilkenny were invited to play in the annual Whit Weekend Wembley Tournament with Tipperary, the winners of a qualifier game, as opposition. In a tough but entertaining game, Tipperary won by 1-10 to 0-7.

A feature of the game were the full-blooded exchanges between Cha and Sean McLoughlin, Tipperary's chief goalscorer and serial tormentor of goalkeepers everywhere. Such was the intensity of the battle between them that they were both sent to the line in the second half. The dismissal had immediate consequences for Cha in relation to maintaining his place on the team. The one-month suspension that followed caused him to miss Kilkenny's hard-fought win over Tipperary later that month in New York in the somewhat pretentiously titled 'World Cup' Final, and the Leinster semi-final win over Wexford. He was back on the panel for the Leinster final but did not make the starting fifteen.

As Kilkenny prepared for the All-Ireland final against Tipperary the tide of public opinion within the county was that, if the title was to be retained a serious overhaul of the team, particularly the full-back line was necessary. Clearly the selectors were of a similar view as, when the team for the final was announced, Cha was positioned at right corner-back, Pa Dillon at full-back, with Fan Larkin at left corner-back. Jim Treacy was the player to lose out. Inexplicably, Seamus Cleere, the 'Hurler of the Year' in 1963, and one of the classiest wing backs the game has seen, was selected at right half-forward.

The match statistics do not provide pleasant reading for Kilkenny followers, even at this remove, as Kilkenny incurred their heaviest All-Ireland final defeat since 1937, losing by 5-13 to 2-8. The followers were merciless in their criticism of the team's performance, with the full-back line, and an unlikely target, goalkeeper Ollie Walsh, attracting most of the censure. That Tipperary's five goals, all from play, some of which were of the 'soft' variety, were scored by their full-forward line gave the followers criticism some additional legitimacy. It must be acknowledged in mitigation, however, that such was Tipperary's dominance in most outfield positions that it was only to be expected that it was the last line of defence, including the goalkeeper, that were subjected to the severest pressure, which they were clearly unable to contain. Fan Larkin was the real long-term victim of the selectors immediate cull, not appearing again on a Championship panel until June, 1970. Cha also incurred the selectors' displeasure, having to be content with a place on the substitutes bench until the beginning of the 1965 season, when he disappeared from the panel. The failure of the Kilkenny selectors to return Seamus Cleere to one of the wing-back positions following Martin Coogan's departure through an early injury, raises the question that, perhaps, Kilkenny had as many problems on the line as on the field in that 1964 final.

Cha returned to the panel for the 1966 Championship and was a substitute on the team that won the Leinster title. He did not make the panel for the All-Ireland final, which was not unexpected, as with Pa Dillon operating at full-forward the team had a ready replacement, if necessary.

The final segment of Cha's inter-county career began when he was recalled to the panel that commenced training for the 1967 All-Ireland final. He did not see any action in Kilkenny's tear-inducing win over Tipperary, a game that saw his clubman, Tom Walsh's career cut short following an eye injury, and where another clubman, Ollie Walsh cemented his reputation as the greatest goalkeeper of his era, if not of all time. As champions, Kilkenny were invited to New York to play the hosts in the 'World Cup' Final. Following a two-leg series, Kilkenny emerged winners with Cha seeing action in both games. On his return from that trip he won his last inter-county medal as a second-half replacement in Kilkenny's Oireachtas Tournament final win over Clare. That successful year of 1967 marked Cha's last association with inter-county hurling.

At club level Cha experienced no major success. Despite having Ollie Walsh, Tom Walsh and Cha available, including an impressive array of exceptionally talented club hurlers, Thomastown remained one of the main under-achieving clubs in the county. However, 1967 appeared as the year in which they would finally realise their undoubted potential. They were impressive in all their Championship games and were given a reasonable chance to divest Bennetsbridge of their county title. Sadly, the injury Tom Walsh suffered in the All-Ireland final, an injury that forced his premature retirement from the game at 23 years of age, proved fatal to Thomastown's chances. In the county final they were only a shadow of the team of earlier games and, without their best outfield player, were soundly beaten. A further opportunity to win a senior title to that generation of Thomastown would not present itself.

Following his original return from England in 1962, Cha secured employment with Roadstone, a company that proved to be a generous employer in the south Kilkenny area, particularly to those with hurling connections. In later years, Cha ran a very successful tarmacadam contracting business with his sons, John and Declan.

On December 2, 1989, Cha, his wife, Babs, and the Whelan family, comprising Declan, Lynda, Berni, Ursula and Joan suffered the ultimate heartbreak with the death of John in a tragic accident. Further sadness visited the Whelan family when Cha died suddenly on March 22, 1996, while following his other passion, greyhound racing, at Kilkenny Greyhound Track.

While Cha's tenure as Kilkenny's Championship full-back was short, it can be summarised as one of 'cometh the hour, cometh the man'. With little or no inter-county experience he was thrust into the white heat of a Leinster semi-final with defeat staring his team in the face. He did the business and, having helped to secure an unlikely win, he performed his onerous defensive duties in similar fashion in the Leinster and All-Ireland successes that soon followed. No doubt, were it not for return to favour of Pa Dillon, and the emergence of Jim Lynch, Cha would have held down a more regular spot as

Kilkenny's full-back. Despite the somewhat patchwork nature of his career, Cha Whelan and his family can be justifiably proud of his contribution to Kilkenny hurling. His position as Kilkenny's seventh All-Ireland winning full-back is well written.

CAREER HIGHLIGHTS

All-Ireland senior finalist: 1963, 1964 and 1967 (s)

All-Ireland senior winner: 1963 and 1967 (s)

Leinster senior winner: 1963, 1964, and 1966(s)

All-Ireland intermediate finalist: 1962 (London)

Oireachtas Tournament winner: 1967

Walsh Cup winner: 1963

London senior Championship winner: 1962 (Sean McDermott's)

Wembley Tournament finalist: 1964

World Cup winner: 1964 (suspended), 1967

All-Ireland junior inter-firm winner: 1975 (Roadstone)

Kilkenny senior county finalist: 1967

American tours: 1964 and 1967

ALL-IRELAND WINNING TEAMS

1963

September 1

Kilkenny 4-17 Waterford 6-8

Croke Park

Attendance 73,123

Kilkenny: Ollie Walsh (Thomastown), Fan Larkin (Eire Og), Cha Whelan (Thomastown), Martin Treacy (Bennettsbridge), Seamus Cleere, captain (Bennettsbridge), Ted Carroll (Lisdowney), Martin Coogan (Erin's Own), Paddy Moran (Bennettsbridge), Sean Clohosey, (Young Ireland, Dublin), Denis Heaslip (Knocktopher), Johnny McGovern (Bennettsbridge), Eddie Keher (The Rower-Inistioge), Tom Walsh (Thomastown), Billy Dwyer (Faughs, Dublin), Tom Murphy (The Rower-Inistioge).

Sub: Oliver Gough (Thomastown) replaced McGovern (injured 45 mins), Tony Kelly (Bennettsbridge), Pa Dillon (St Lachtain's), Sean Buckley (St Lachtain's), Willie Murphy (Slieverue), Alfie Hickey (St Lachtain's), Timmy Kelly (Bennettsbridge), Noel Skehan (Bennettsbridge), Jim Treacy (Bennettsbrdge).

PART TWO

Those Who Still Live to Tell the Tale

Dillon

St Lachtain's Pa Dillon, seen here in 1972 All-Ireland winning team photo (back row, third from left), reigned supreme against full-forwards of all sizes and abilities. He hurled against such greats as Tony Doran, Mackey McKenna, Ray Cummins, Sean McLoughlin, Roger Ryan and Jack Berry.

chapter 8

"I met Jack Rochford once, when I was about 12 years of age.

It was after the fair in Kilkenny and I went with my father to O'Connell's pub, then owned by Jimmy O'Connell, Kilkenny's All-Ireland winning goalkeeper of 1935 and 1939. It was a GAA house and there were always a few famous hurlers around the place, particularly on busy days or match days in the city.

I was excited afterwards when my father told me that the man I had just met had won several All-Ireland medals with Kilkenny.

From my earliest days, I always operated in the full-back line, usually at full-back. As a youth, I would have seen 'Diamond' Hayden and 'Link' Walsh in action, many times.

Those players were then living legends around the county.

My inter-county career covered two periods, one very brief, the other lasting as long as I could possibly make it. Shortly after making my debut in the spring of 1960, I played in the Leinster final, which we lost to Wexford. The entire experience was over so quickly that I probably didn't benefit much from it.

I rejoined the panel in August 1963, and, except for a short break in the spring of 1973, remained a member until after that year's All-Ireland final.

While I was always aware of Kilkenny's tradition in the game, and my own responsibilities as a county representative, I could never allow any other issues to distract me when I was playing. Apart from attempting to play my part for the team as best I could my other personal ambition was simply to keep my position on the team.

The game was too fast and competitive to carry any extra baggage. Without full concentration on the job at hand, a player would be submerged by the occasion and risk never being heard of again.

Remember that your direct opponent had the same mindset and ideals. It was only in retirement that the historical aspects arose.

From 1964 a genuine, competitive team began to come together. Players such as Pat Henderson, Jim Treacy, John Teehan and Claus Dunne, began to assert themselves, while Tom Walsh was beginning to dominate games like he did in his minor days. While we experienced bad days against Tipperary in big Croke Park games, we were gradually getting their measure in other games, and the fear factor was lessening all the time.

Our win over them in the 1967 All-Ireland final was the result of many hard lessons learned along the way.

I never carried any fears of getting injured at any time during my career. As already said, my main ambition was to play to the very best of my ability for the team. My selfish ambition was simply to keep my place. While I was first-choice full-back for the main part, I was always aware that one or two careless outings would quickly bring the end.

The one big nagging fear that I did have, and the longer my career lasted the more pronounced it became, was of being totally outplayed on some big occasion in Croke Park. The longer the playing career, the more inevitable that such a day is around the corner.

I feel that this is the fear that ultimately leads most long-serving players into retirement. I loved hurling and wished I could have played on, but it just wasn't possible. However, to have fronted Ollie Walsh for so long, and to have played with such hurling giants as Ted Carroll, Seamus Cleere, Martin Coogan, Paddy Moran, Frank Cummins, Eddie Keher, Pat Delaney, Tom Walsh and so many others was more than ample compensation."

Pa Dillon

—〰—

Pa Dillon played senior Championship hurling for Kilkenny for the first time in 1960, and for the last time in 1972. In most of the intervening years he was consistently a central figure in many memorable Kilkenny Championship successes. While not wishing to diminish the role which he played in those successes, or the longevity of his career, one incident occurred during that career which, while it took no longer then a second or so to execute, bestowed on him the eternal gratitude of all Kilkenny followers, particularly those lucky to have witnessed it.

The year was 1967, the date September 3, the venue Croke Park.

As the clock showed ten minutes or so remaining, the All-Ireland final was entering its critical stage. Kilkenny, having erased Tipperary's six-point, half-time lead, had eased out in front by three points. But battle-hardened Tipperary were not about to surrender easily and were still a major threat to Kilkenny's craving to lay that much hyped, but difficult to ignore, 'Tipperary Hoodoo'.

Following a threatening Tipperary attack, Pa found he faced a dilemma, one which demanded both immediate evaluation and reaction. Tipperary's Donie Nealon had soloed unhindered to the Kilkenny 21-yard line, with his colleague Liam Devaney standing unmarked on the edge of the Kilkenny square. Pa was the sole Kilkenny defender in close proximity.

His options were limited, with all the advantages favouring Nealon. However, Pa's defender's instinct told him that Nealon would most likely attempt a lofted pass inside to the unmarked Devaney, rather than continue on his own. Thus, when Nealon did as Pa had anticipated, the Freshford man was primed. Stretching his long 6' 2" frame to its optimum, and with his hurley aloft, Pa judged the trajectory of the pass perfectly. He stopped the ball in flight, brought it down to ground level, completing the manoeuvre with a telling clearance. What would most certainly have been a Tipperary goal and, perhaps, a game-altering one, was transformed into a probable All-Ireland-winning interception. How fitting that it was Pa, a folk hero to Kilkenny followers, who had executed such a crucial piece of action – one that helped to create the win that changed the course of Kilkenny hurling.

Pa was born in October, 1938, to Robert and Catherine Dillon (nee Farrell, from Clinstown) a farming family from Bawntanameenagh, Freshford. In addition to Pa, the Dillons had four other children, William, Cecelia, Angela and Kitty. Robert Dillon was a keen hurling follower and rarely missed a game, whether at club or county level. Such was his commitment to the game that, for many years before the local St Lachtain's club acquired their own grounds, Robert was only too willing to allow the club the use of one of his fields for both training and games. Formed in 1951, St Lachtain's took its name from a fourth-century saint who originated in Donoughmore, Co Cork, but who spent most of his religious life in the Freshford area.

Through the influence and drive of local primary school teacher, Tom Waldron, Freshford began to make their mark at underage hurling, winning the 1951 Under-14 Roinn B, the club's first underage success. That year Pa's potential was recognised with selection on the county Under-14 team, where one of his colleagues was Ollie Walsh, then the most talked about underage hurling prospect in the county. Over the following 20 years or so, Pa and Ollie's respective careers would both collide with, and complement, each other's very prominently at club, county and inter-provincial level.

The club's attention towards youth development was further rewarded in 1954 with an Under-16 county title win. The club, known as St Lachtain's from Under-16 upwards, cemented its growing reputation as a future hurling stronghold by qualifying for the county minor finals of 1954, 1955 and 1956. Pa's displays during the successful 1955 campaign earned him selection on that year's county minor panel, which won the Leinster Championship. He won his second provincial medal the following year as the team's first-choice full-back, but later endured the disappointment of defeat by Tipperary in the All-Ireland final.

For the next few years, Pa's hurling exploits were limited to the white heat of the Northern junior Championship, an experience that was to prove very beneficial when he eventually graduated to the extremely combative, high-octane senior inter-county stage.

Pa's next taste of inter-county hurling was in 1959 with the Kilkenny junior team, alternating between full-back and left corner-back in their unsuccessful provincial campaign. At club level that year Pa was an inspirational figure in St Lachtain's county junior title win, defeating an Ollie Walsh-led Thomastown in the final. That final, played in March, 1960, was timely for Pa in regard to the development of his career as, in the absence through injury of Jim 'Link' Walsh, he was drafted onto the panel for pre-Championship tournament and challenge games. His biggest test came in Kilkenny's Whit Weekend Wembley Tournament win over All-Ireland champions, Waterford.

Pa survived, but sportingly admits that he was almost submerged by the intensity and speed of the game. He held his place for Kilkenny's Leinster Championship win over Westmeath, and subsequent Leinster final defeat by Wexford. Though he played well in that Wexford game, where his duel with teak-tough full-forward Jack Harding was a feature of the game, Pa's name would not again appear on a Kilkenny Championship panel until August, 1963.

Meanwhile, St Lachtain's continued to prosper, especially following the unification of the two clubs in the parish, St Lachtain's and Threecastles. Two senior county titles were won, in 1961 and 1963, with Pa the driving force behind both wins. The 1961 win was memorable in that it was achieved against a, high-quality Near South side, led by Ollie Walsh, that were considered short odds favourites to win.

Following Kilkenny's 1963 Leinster final win, Pa was called into the panel that went into training for the All-Ireland final. Though he did not play any part in Kilkenny's win, Pa's long-term association with Kilkenny was on course, an association that would see him play in six All-Ireland finals, five of them from the full-back position.

Having been introduced as a half-time substitute in Kilkenny's Oireachtas Cup semi-final defeat by Tipperary in September, 1963, Pa remained as the team's first-choice full-back throughout the 1963-64 National League campaign. He missed the 1964 Leinster semi-final win over Wexford through injury, but was on duty for the remainder of the Championship. Following Kilkenny's 14-point mauling in the All-Ireland final, Pa was the only member of the full-back line to escape the selectors' cull. His retention was subsequently justified by his selection on that year's All-Star team.

However, 1965 was a traumatic year for Kilkenny, losing the finals of the National League, Leinster Championship, Oireachtas Tournament and Walsh Cup. The Kilkenny hurling public were now demanding that a more physical approach be adopted, particularly amongst the forwards, if the slide that the team was experiencing was ever to be arrested. In an attempt to add some badly needed strength and steel to the forward line, the selectors moved Pa to full forward, replacing him at full-back with Mooncoin's Jimmy Lynch.

By the middle years of the decade, that Kilkenny team had reached a crossroads in their development. They were clearly the country's second-best team, but were still a long way off the ruthless, efficient, winning outfit that their nemesis, Tipperary, had become. Over a two-year period, Tipperary had handed heavy defeats in one All-Ireland final, one National League final, and two Oireachtas Tournament finals. Kilkenny's return from other clashes with Tipperary during those years were a World Cup win in New York, a Wembley Tournament win, and a meaningless National League win in Thurles, hardly comparable achievements. A clearly identifiable sphere of rancour and spite had developed between the teams and supporters at a level that was unprecedented at inter-county level anywhere in the country. Even in faraway venues such as Wembley Stadium and New York's Gaelic Park, the players found it impossible to resist the temptation to both settle old scores and open fresh ones.

Kilkenny people were pragmatic enough to accept that Tipperary were clearly the better team. The match results could not be denied. What was difficult to digest was the hubris with which Tipperary appeared, in Kilkenny's eyes, to display in relation to hurling in general, and their relationship with Kilkenny in particular. Over the years Kilkenny had sportingly accepted recurring periods of playing second fiddle to Cork, Limerick, Waterford and, more recently, to Wexford. With Tipperary, however, there was no such goodwill. To say there was a shared antipathy would not even closely describe it.

In John Harrington's excellent biography of John Doyle, *Doyle: The Greatest Hurling Story Ever Told*, Mick Burns, Tipperary's mild-mannered wing back of the '60s remarked that playing Kilkenny was different to playing Cork or Wexford. "Cork and Wexford were sportsmen," Burns remarked. "Playing Kilkenny was different. It was pure bitter."

Some few years ago, Babs Keating, a Tipperary forward of those years, was quoted, unsportingly, as saying: "In my time, Kilkenny were beaten as soon as they saw the blue and gold jersey." Pa would, in time, change Keating's tune.

It was clear, therefore, that only a win over Tipperary in a National final at Croke Park would restore to Kilkenny the credibility the whole county craved. It duly arrived in May 1966 when, in a tremendous game played in wet and windy conditions at Croke Park, Kilkenny overturned their tormentors in the 'Home' final (0-9 to 0-7). The win was greeted with more relief than elation.

While Kilkenny's score tally was modest, what was significant was that the defence held what was regarded as one of the most potent forward lines of all times to a losing score of a meagre seven points. Kilkenny played that day with both a ferocity and a ruthlessness that had previously been the hallmark of Tipperary. What both surprised and pleased Kilkenny supporters was that, when this ferocity and ruthlessness was employed, Tipperary accepted it and were duly beaten. The spell had been broken. The seeds sown by that win would reap a rich harvest in September, 1967.

The experiment of playing Pa at full-forward throughout 1966 was, in the main, a success. In March, he was one of Leinster's best performers in their two-point defeat by Munster in the Railway Cup final. In addition to playing a vital part in the League final win, Pa also led the line in the recapture of the Leinster title. His pending clash with Cork's abrasive Tom O'Donoghue in the All-Ireland final was eagerly awaited.

However, what turned out to be Pa's last appearance as Kilkenny's Championship full-forward was a bitter disappointment for both player and his team. As the form team, Kilkenny entered that All-Ireland final as clear favourites against a very inexperienced Cork outfit. However, Kilkenny's subsequent shock defeat following their very dispirited performance was heavily criticised at local level.

Amongst the many issues that proved controversial was the first-half substitution of Pa, a move that was neither justified, nor of any benefit to the team. Shortly after the All-Ireland final, he played full-forward in Kilkenny's defeat of New York in the National League final proper, scoring two goals. In the space of two September weekends Pa's full-forward career had run its course.

By the start of the 1966/67 National League in October, Pa was restored to the full-back position, with Jimmy Lynch making the reverse journey. From then, until he retired, Pa's tenure as Kilkenny's Championship full-back remained unchallenged. He played in four further All-Ireland finals, winning three. He became a serial winner of Leinster Championships, Oireachtas Tournament, Railway Cup and Walsh Cup medals. Suspension, following a sending off in a National League game against Tipperary in March, ruled him out of the 1967 Railway Cup final, which Leinster won.

However, Kilkenny's subsequent All-Ireland final win over Tipperary, and his subjugation in that game of Babs Keating, the other player involved in the sending-off incident, was more than ample compensation.

Pa's timely interception of Nealon's menacing lofted pass in that 1967 final was only one of the numerous passages of play executed by him that helped to bring about that epochal win. In the finals of 1963, 1964 and 1966, Kilkenny conceded a total of 14 goals and 30 points. That the scores against column in the 1967 final read a mere two goals and seven points, against one of the most potent attacking combinations the game has seen, was testament to Kilkenny's ruthless, but lawful defending.

Only the naive would have failed to recognise that the 1967 final was not spared flashes of the bitterness that so characterised most of the recent meetings between the teams. Lots of festering sores were settled, but the loss of Kilkenny's two foremost forwards, Tom Walsh and Eddie Keher, to second-half injuries ensured that the next important meeting between the sides would be a flinty affair. The National League final the following April would not be for the faint-hearted. And it wasn't.

Pa always regarded Railway Cup selection as an immense honour, and reserved possibly his greatest ever Croke Park performance for the 1965 Railway Cup final. Fronting Ollie Walsh, and flanked by two hard-tackling Wexfordmen, Tom Neville and Ned Colfer, Pa was in unbeatable form. Munster, bolstered by no fewer than ten of Tipperary's 1964 All-Ireland winning team, tried a succession of players on Pa but to no avail as he continued to hurl defiantly in one of Leinster's most memorable wins. Pa is saddened at the decline of the inter-provincial series, and feels that instead of being phased out, every effort should be made to revive them.

For Pa, 1968 was another very unrewarding year as he found himself on the losing side in the finals of the Railway Cup, National League and Leinster Championship. He was extremely shocked at the totally unjust six-month suspension imposed on Ollie Walsh by the Central Council following their kangaroo-court style inquiry into incidents which marred that year's National League final with Tipperary, where, once again, the enmity between the teams was very evident.

In 1969, Pa won his third All-Ireland medal, his second at full-back, in Kilkenny's win over Cork. Having played poorly in the opening half, Kilkenny regrouped to dominate the remainder of the game, running out comfortable winners by a six-point margin. That game saw the first instalment of the many memorable duels between Pa and Cork's towering full forward, Ray Cummins. A final audit of their encounters would be estimated as a 50-50 split, a result that should satisfy both players.

Pa's next attempt at further All-Ireland success, 1971, ended in bitter disappointment. A new-look Tipperary team, whose unheralded forward line breached what had been regarded as an impregnable Kilkenny defence for five goals, took the All-Ireland title by a three-point margin. Kilkenny's lacklustre display, particularly that of the defence, including goalkeeper Ollie Walsh, came in for much adverse comment. That Kilkenny would go on to win three of the next four All-Ireland finals, while Tipperary would not again win even another Munster title for 16 years, illustrates the lost opportunity that was 1971.

Whatever sense of bewilderment and despair the Kilkenny players and followers felt with the events of 1971 were spectacularly banished the following September. A remarkable final 20-minute scoring blitz enabled Kilkenny to take their 18th title, leaving Cork, once again, wondering at Kilkenny's ability to win All-Ireland finals when least expected to. The Kilkenny defence as a unit were outplayed by a fast- moving Cork attack for practically two-thirds of the game, by which time they had built up a lead of 5-11 to 1-15. Inspired by Pat Henderson, Pa, and sub Martin Coogan, the defence suddenly, as if on the turn of a switch, regrouped to totally, eclipse the Cork attack, holding them scoreless for the remaining 20 minutes of the game. The Kilkenny forwards, menacingly led by Pat Delaney, responded greedily, hoovering up an unanswered two goals and nine points, to record one of Kilkenny's most memorable wins.

This game was Pa's last association as a player with both the pressures and pleasures of All-Ireland Sunday. His tally of four Celtic Crosses, three as a player, was more than a reasonable return by a man who was what can be described as a 'late developer'.

Pa played in the pre-Christmas 1972–1973 National League games but did not appear in the competition's latter stages. However, he was re-called to the panel for the commencement of the 1973 Championship, but did not feature in any of Kilkenny's games. He did, however, play in Kilkenny's Walsh Cup final win over Wexford in August, a game that was, in essence, a final trial for the All-Ireland final against Limerick. There were calls for his inclusion on the injury-ravaged team for the All-Ireland final, but the selectors were not swayed, staying with the incumbent Nicky Orr. Pa retired quietly from inter-county hurling over the following winter. He continued to play club hurling well into his 40s.

Unlike many of his contemporaries who do not support the modern-day approach to virtual year-round training routines, Pa remarked: "I would be thrilled to be playing at present where every effort is made to improve the fitness and skills levels of the players. Every sportsperson, irrespective of their chosen sport, should avail of every opportunity to embrace new training routines so as to develop and improve all aspects of their sport. If not, why bother to participate at all?"

Considering the tremendously successful career he experienced, one is tempted to ask why did it take him so long to become established?

Pa availed of our meeting to dispel a widely-held view that he held an intense dislike for Tipperary people and their hurlers. "Nothing could be further from the truth," he emphasised, "I have a huge respect for Tipperary people, both on and off the field. In all my hectic battles with them over the years not once was I ever the victim of any personal remarks from any of their players or officials. Neither did I encounter any animosity within the county during my many years doing business there as an oil company agent. Tipperary are great hurlers, great people."

While rarely a direct opponent, Pa acknowledges that Jimmy Doyle was one of the game's icons. "He wielded the hurley like a magic wand," remarked Pa.

Notwithstanding Pa's stated equanimity towards Tipperary and its people, given the intensity with which he played against them, and indeed against all Munster teams, perhaps there is a certain irony in that the name of his townland; Bawnteenameenagh translates into 'the fields of the Munster men'.

Pa's hurling talents have been inherited by his daughter, Gillian, and nephew, Aidan Fogarty, who are both multiple All-Ireland medallists with Kilkenny at various grades in camogie and hurling.

Pa is grateful to hurling for the many opportunities it afforded him to play the game in such places as New York's Gaelic Park, Wembley Stadium, San Francisco and Chicago, and to visit many famous places.

Though very tall and of slight build, Pa had great strength and was extremely difficult to dislodge under a high ball. He was a fearless competitor and was a far more accomplished hurler than first impressions might indicate. "Pa Dillon was the one Kilkenny player that Tipperary were genuinely afraid of," noted John Harrington, in his biography of John Doyle.

Throughout his long career, whether at club, county or inter-provincial level, Pa rarely encountered an easy opponent, invariably coming into contact with the opposition's best or second-best forward. Household names, such as Tony Doran, Mackey McKenna, Ray Cummins, Sean McLoughlin, Roger Ryan and Jack Berry were the calibre of the players Pa faced on a regular basis. Life was never carefree on the edge of Pa's square. He would not have wished it otherwise.

The extended Dillon family have experienced some memorable days following Pa's hurling exploits. The family have, however, also witnessed very dark days due to the untimely deaths of Pa and Billy's three sisters, Cecelia Gorman, Kitty Fogarty and Angela Murphy, while all relatively young women.

Pa resides at Bawntanameenagh, Freshford, with his wife, Theresa. They have two children, Bobby and Gillian. During his working life, Pa combined farming with sales duties for Top Oil, a Kilkenny-based oil company.

CAREER HIGHLIGHTS

All-Ireland senior finalist: 1963(s), 1964, 1966, 1967, 1969, 1971, 1972, and 1973(s)
All-Ireland senior winner: 1963(s), 1967, 1969 and 1972
Leinster senior winner: 1964, 1966, 1967, 1969, 1971, 1972 and 1973(s)
National League winner: 1965-66
Railway Cup winner: 1965, 1967 (missed final) and 1972
Oireachtas Tournament winner: 1966, 1967 and 1969

Wembley Tournament winner: 1960 and 1965

Walsh Cup winner: 1963, 1970 and 1973

All-Star Awards: 1964 and 1967

Leinster minor winner: 1955 and 1956

Kilkenny senior Championship: 1961 and 1963

Kilkenny junior Championship: 1959

Kilkenny minor Championship: 1955

Kilkenny U-16 Championship: 1954

Kilkenny U-14 Championship: 1951

American tours: 1964, 1967, 1969 and 1972

ALL-IRELAND WINNING TEAMS

1967
September 3
Kilkenny 3-8 Tipperary 2-7
Croke Park
Attendance 64,241

Kilkenny: Ollie Walsh (Thomastown), Ted Carroll (Lisdowney), Pa Dillon (St Lachtain's), Jim Treacy, captain (Bennettsbridge), Seamus Cleere (Bennettsbridge), Pat Henderson (The Fenians), Martin Coogan (Erin's Own), Paddy Moran (Bennettsbridge), John Teehan (St Lachtain's), Eddie Keher (The Rower-Inistioge), Tom Walsh (Thomastown), Claus Dunne (Mooncoin), Jim Bennett (Bennettsbridge), Jim Lynch (Mooncoin), Martin Brennan (Erin's Own).

Subs: Noel Skehan (Bennettsbridge), Cha Whelan (Thomastown), Pat Carroll (Knocktopher), replaced Tom Walsh (injured, 56 mins), John Kinsella (Bennettsbridge), replaced Bennett (57 mins), Dick Blanchfield (Lisdowney) replaced Keher (injured, 43 mins), Frank Cummins (Knocktopher), Patsy Foley (Clara).

1969
September 7
Kilkenny 2-15 Cork 2-9
Croke Park
Attendance 66,844

Kilkenny: Ollie Walsh (Thomastown), Ted Carroll (Lisdowney), Pa Dillon (St Lachtain's), Jim Treacy (Bennettsbridge), Billy Murphy (The Rower-Inistioge), Pat Henderson (The Fenians), Martin Coogan (Erin's Own), Mick Lalor (Coon), Frank Cummins (Blackrock, Cork), Claus Dunne (Mooncoin), Pat Delaney (The Fenians), Eddie Keher, captain (The Rower-Inistioge), Joe Millea (Graigue), Martin Brennan (Erin's Own), Tom Murphy (The Rower-Inistioge).

Subs: Paddy Moran* (Bennettsbridge) replaced Delaney (injured, 41mins), Pat Kavanagh (The Rower-Inistioge and UCD), replaced Dunne (25 mins), Jim Lynch (Mooncoin), Seamus Cleere (Bennettsbridge), Noel Skehan (Bennettsbridge), Sean Buckley (Moindearg, Dublin) replaced Tom Murphy (54 mins). *Paddy Moran was selected to start at midfield but withdrew due to illness. He was replaced by Mick Lalor.

1972
September 3 (80-minute game)
Kilkenny 3-24 Cork 5-11
Croke Park
Attendance 66,135

Kilkenny: Noel Skehan, captain (Bennettsbridge), Fan Larkin (James Stephens), Pa Dillon (St Lachtain's), Jim Treacy (Bennettsbridge), Pat Lawlor (Bennettsbridge), Pat Henderson (The Fenians), Eamonn Morrissey (James Stephens), Frank Cummins (Blackrock, Cork), Liam 'Chunky' O'Brien (James Stephens), Mick Crotty (James Stephens), Pat Delaney (The Fenians), John Kinsella (Bennettsbridge), Ned Byrne (James Stephens), Kieran Purcell (Windgap), Eddie Keher (The Rower-Inistioge).

Sub: Ollie Walsh (Thomastown United), Nicky Orr (The Fenians), Mossie Murphy (Mullinavat) replaced Byrne (half time), Martin Coogan (Erin's Own) replaced Larkin (injured, 50 mins), Senan Cooke (St Senan's), Paddy Moran (Bennettsbridge) replaced Kinsella (75 mins).

Orr

Nicky Orr's father, Joe, hailed from Glencar, Co Donegal. He came to the Kilkenny area as an army recruit in the early 1940s, during 'The Emergency', and is possibly the only man with a Church of Ireland background to have a son to captain an All-Ireland winning hurling team.

chapter 9

"When I joined the Kilkenny panel in 1971 I had no idea where it would all lead. My rewards from hurling at that point were meagre, by any standard. My ambitions were equally modest.

The main target of my efforts was in the direction of my club, which had won its first senior county title the previous October.

However, I became a sub to Pa Dillon throughout the inter-county Championships of 1971 and 1972, winning an All-Ireland medal the latter year. While not playing any part in Kilkenny's Championship runs either year, I did succeed in playing several National League and Tournament games, occupying all three full back line positions, as the occasion's demanded. These experiences would stand to me later when I became a regular.

Pa took time over the winter of 1972–1973 to decide if he was going to make himself available for the 1973 Championship. When he did return to the panel the selectors kept faith with me and I remained first choice full back for the following four Championship campaigns.

They were four memorable years during which Kilkenny contested three All-Ireland finals, winning two. We went on two tours to the United States, and won the National League title in 1976.

Even though I had no inter-county Championship experience when facing into the 1973 campaign I was not overawed as I had faced many of the country's full forwards in National League games during my first two years on the panel. What also helped greatly was that the Kilkenny Championship at that time was very competitive, where the standard of opposition full forwards was extremely high.

Coming face to face, regularly with players such as Georgie Leahy, Ned Byrne, Tommy Malone, Claus Dunne, Mick Crotty, John Kinsella, Paddy Treacy, Eddie Keher, or our own Pat Delaney in club training sessions, were ideal tests for the inter-county scene.

Also, as The Fenians began to be invited to play tournament games around the country and to participate in the club Championship I was competing against many of the players I was meeting at inter-county level. All those tests helped greatly as my inter-county career developed.

My last Championship game for Kilkenny was a difficult afternoon. We were demolished by 17 points by Wexford in the 1976 Leinster final. I was, at the time, suffering from a serious knee injury and withdrew from consideration from the county team prior to the commencement of the 1976-77 National League.

I had not experienced an eventful underage career so it was a great honour to be selected for the senior team. That most of the players I was joining up with were already well-established, successful players was intimidating on the one hand, while on the other hand their experience helped me settle in quite easily.

It is only since I retired that I can fully appreciate the extent of our team's achievements and great honour it was to follow in the footsteps of so many hurling legends. When you are playing you are not concerned with anything other than the next match, your next opponent, playing well, and keeping your place. They are sufficient motivational issues to be getting on with."

Nicky Orr

—◇—

Nicky Orr first joined the Kilkenny panel in 1971. As Pa Dillon's understudy, he saw no immediate Championship action, his appearances being limited to National League, Walsh Cup and tournament games. However, by the spring of 1973, Pa's long-term plans were still on hold, enabling Nicky to cement his place as first choice full-back. When Pa did return to the panel in May of that year for pre-Championship training he was unable to dislodge Nicky who had by then satisfied all the selectors' requirements. During his tenure as first choice full-back Nicky played in three All-Ireland finals, winning two, one as captain.

Nicky's father, Joe, hailed from Glencar, Co Donegal. He came to the Kilkenny area as an Army recruit in the early 1940s during 'The Emergency'. Joe later married Theresa Grace, from Johnstown, where the young couple eventually set up home. Joe is possibly the only man with a Church of Ireland background to have a son to captain an All-Ireland winning hurling team.

Nicky attended National School in Johnstown with whom he played schools hurling. He later progressed to the Johnstown Under-16, minor and Under-21 teams without any memorable successes. A defeat in the Northern Under-21 final of 1967 was the pinnacle of his club's underage achievements. However, his displays in that campaign earned him selection on the county Under-21 team for the 1968 Championship, which ended in an All-Ireland final defeat by Cork.

At that time all underage hurling in the parish was played with the Johnstown parish team. However, there were two separate adult clubs in the parish, Beggar St Finbarr's, with whom Nicky played, and Johnstown St Kieran's. Neither club demonstrated the potential that they could progress from junior to senior level in the immediate future. There was no intermediate grade in vogue at the time .

The relative success of the Johnstown Under-21 team in 1967 prompted certain influential members of the local hurling fraternity to bring about the unification of the two hurling units in the parish. Thus, in March, 1968, St Finbarr's and St Kieran's were disbanded and The Fenians were formed, a development that altered, in the best possible manner, the landscape of hurling, both in the parish and throughout the county. It is doubtful if those behind the unification had the remotest intimation as to how successful their creation would become.

The wisdom of unification was immediately justified when The Fenians won the county junior Championship in their first year in existence and were automatically promoted senior. They were the surprise packets of the 1969 senior Championship, and, with the momentum behind them, they qualified for the county final. However, whatever excess feelings of satisfaction they may have felt as to their rapid rate of progress were quickly shattered when, in April, 1970, in the delayed County final, The Fenians were totally over-run by a resurgent James Stephens by a 16-point margin.

One of the many factors in that defeat was the total eclipse of The Fenians' highly regarded full-back line whose direct opponents accounted for six of their team's eight goals. Yet, almost incredibly, when both teams met within six months in the 1970 County final, The Fenians reversed that result to take their first senior title. On this occasion it was their full-back line who were the masters, completely dominating their patch and their opponents to lay the foundations for one of the Championship's most astonishing results. County player Pat Henderson and Nicky were the men who set the standard for The Fenians' defiance from the first whistle, a standard that was feverishly maintained until the long whistle blew. If for no other reason, that win marked out The Fenians as special, but there was better to come.

In total, one junior title, five senior titles and one provincial title were acquired during The Fenians' glory days. When in full flight they were an awesome sight and were almost unbeatable. They played with an air of confidence that bordered on haughtiness. This writer had the privilege of playing against them on a few occasions, and to say that I enjoyed limited possession of the ball would be a gross overstatement. Physically strong in all pivotal positions, and with the full fifteen being exceptionally good hurlers, they were a formidable challenge for any club with their own Championship aspirations. They dominated club hurling throughout the early and mid-1970s.

That period, from the late 1960s to the late 1970s was one when the senior Championship was arguably at its most competitive and most compelling. Championship games between The Fenians, serial winners Bennettsbridge, 1968 champions The Rower-Inistioge, and 1969 champions, James Stephens, drew attendances from far and wide to Nowlan Park, where the fare on offer was invariably of a far higher quality than that at most inter-county games of the same era. Thus, when Nicky was called up to the county panel in 1971, he had served a tough apprenticeship , and was more than ready for the challenge.

While Pat Delaney and Pat Henderson were the marquee names on any Fenians' team sheet, to regular watchers of the team, and opponents, their next most valuable player was undoubtedly Nicky. Very strongly built, endowed with unwavering courage, Nicky possessed a totally uncomplicated, dependable technique, one that invariably held firm, irrespective of the pressures. Curiously he was one of the few Kilkenny players of recent times to experience a successful senior inter-county career without the background of a similarly successful colleges and or minor career.

As noted, Nicky's initial two years on the panel saw him limited to non-Championship playing time. In the absence of the regular incumbents he frequently saw action in all three full-back-line positions. He eventually made his Championship debut in Kilkenny's reasonably comfortable 1973 Leinster semi-final win over Dublin.

His first serious test came in that year's Leinster final where he came face to face with Wexford's Tony Doran, then one of game's foremost goal scorers. Doran was to his generation of Wexford players and followers what Nicky Rackard had been in the 1950s, and had almost single-handedly led Wexford to the 1968 All-Ireland title. Yet, when the final whistle blew to signal the end of that Leinster final, Nicky had conceded neither scores nor frees to Wexford's leader. However, no sooner had Nicky sampled that initial success than, in his debut All-Ireland, he endured the flip-side of sport as an injury-ravaged Kilkenny lost the final to a highly motivated, all-action Limerick.

Nicky's next Championship season saw him reach the pinnacle of his career. Having retained the provincial title following a nerve-wracking 6-13 to 2-24 win over Wexford in the Leinster final, Kilkenny were back in the All-Ireland final, with their conquerors of the previous year, Limerick, who were attempting a successful title defence. This time there would be no regrets as Kilkenny comfortably won their 19th title by a 12-point margin. Nicky was now his county's ninth All-Ireland winning full-back, and its 15th winning captain . He was the first player from the northern tip of the county to captain a senior All-Ireland winning team.

Kilkenny successfully defended their Championship titles in 1975, with wins over Wexford and Galway in the respective finals under the captaincy of another Fenians player, Billy Fitzpatrick. The team was then being regarded in some circles as one of the greatest of all time, and were listed as short odds to retain their titles in 1976. Those few pundits who doubted

Kilkenny's ability to keep on winning were duly converted in the late spring of 1976 when the team returned from an energy-sapping tour of the West Coast of America to win the replayed National League final against Clare by a five-goal margin. Having successfully qualified for the Leinster final, only an untried Wexford side stood in the way of Kilkenny's sixth successive All-Ireland final appearance and a tilt at a three-in-a-row of titles. However, in one of the great shock results of the time, Kilkenny were obliterated on a 2-20 to 1-6 scoreline. That Kilkenny scored a mere solitary point in the second half to Wexford's 1-9 is an indication of the extent of their difficulties. Not since Wexford's 5-11 to 0-7 win in the 1954 semi-final had Kilkenny suffered such discomfort in modern-day provincial Championship hurling.

That defeat signalled the end of Nicky's inter-county Championship career. In hindsight, it could be argued that the selectors were somewhat hasty in calling time on him. Over the following five Championships Kilkenny used five different full-backs, Pat Henderson, Fan Larkin, Paddy Prendergast, Brian Cody and Jim Moran – a period which, with the exception of 1979, could not be regarded, by any standards, as being a bountiful one for the county. Nonetheless, while Nicky's career was relatively short in duration it was otherwise in achievements. He won every major that the inter-county game could offer. He also won a Railway Cup medal in 1975, as a substitute, on a particularly strong Leinster team that was in the final act of a successful run that saw them win five consecutive inter-provincial titles.

Nicky's departure from the inter-county scene was as unpretentious as his entrance. There was no public announcement. He returned to club hurling where he continued to play until the early 1980s.

While Nicky was acclimatising himself to the inter-county scene in the early 1970s he was already one of the foundation stones of a very miserly Fenians backline that followed up their inaugural county title win in 1970 with three consecutive titles in 1972, 1973 and 1974. The 1973 win set them apart as an exceptional team. Thirteen points down at one stage in the first half of the County final and 10 points down at the break against a quality James Stephens side heavily decked with inter-county players, the Fenians etched out one of the most extraordinary and thrilling County final fight-backs ever witnessed to retain their title by a four-point margin (7-8 to 5-10).

Nicky was at the forefront of a defence that, while it leaked scores alarmingly in the first-half, succeeded in holding the hitherto free-scoring Stephens attack to a modest second-half score of 1-4, of which only a solitary point came from play.

—◇◇◇—

Following their 1974 County title win, The Fenians became the first Kilkenny club to win the Leinster club Championship. Sadly, they left all their good form behind them in the All-Ireland final against St Finbarr's, losing by eight points. Nicky and his Fenians' comrades would not get a further opportunity for All-Ireland club honours as, when they won their fifth and last county title in 1977, they carelessly lost the subsequent Leinster final to thirteen-man Rathnure team by three points (0-16 to 1-10).

At inter-county level Nicky never attracted the high media attention that followed some of his colleagues, such as Pat Henderson, Fan Larkin, Kieran Purcell or Pat Delaney. Such a low-key approach suited both his game and his personality. Public demonstrations of his commitment to his team, such as jersey-tucking antics or revealing media interviews, were not for him. Nicky's approach on any given day was to clinically assess what had to be done for the team, and then to execute it without pomp or ceremony. His objective was to leave the field of play, whatever the outcome, secure in the knowledge that he had left nothing undone for the benefit of the team. He was the ultimate team player and a loyal servant of both The Fenians and Kilkenny. John Holohan would have approved of the exploits of Johnstown's newest All-Ireland winning full-back.

Nicky, who has been employed by Roadmaster Caravans, Johnstown, for the past 35 years, lives in Ballycuddihy, outside Johnstown with his wife, Mary. They have one daughter, Patricia.

CAREER HIGHLIGHTS

All-Ireland senior finalist: 1971 (s), 1972 (s) 1973, 1974 and 1975

All-Ireland senior winner: 1972 (s), 1974 (Captain) and 1975

Leinster senior winner: 1971, 1972, 1973, 1974 and 1975

All-Ireland U-21 finalist: 1968

Leinster U-21 winner: 1968

Railway Cup winner: 1975

National League winner: 1975-76

Walsh Cup winner: 1970 (played Feb 1972) 1973 and 1974

County senior winner: 1970, 1972, 1973, 1974 and 1977

Leinster club winner: 1974-75

All-Ireland club finalist: 1974-75

County junior winner: 1968

County junior football winner: 1971

All-Ireland Inter-firm winner: 1981 (Building Systems, Johnstown)

American tours: 1973, 1975 and 1976

ALL-IRELAND WINNING TEAMS

1974

September 1

Kilkenny 3-19 Limerick 1-13

Croke Park

Attendance 62,071

Kilkenny: Noel Skehan (Bennettsbridge), Fan Larkin (James Stephens), Nicky Orr (The Fenians), captain, Jim Treacy (Bennettsbridge), Pat Lawlor (Bennettsbridge), Pat Henderson (The Fenians), Tom McCormack (James Stephens), Liam 'Chunky' O'Brien (James Stephens), Frank Cummins (Backrock, Cork), Mick Crotty (James Stephens), Pat Delaney (The Fenians), Billy Fitzpatrick (The Fenians), Mick 'Cloney' Brennan (Erin's Own), Kieran Purcell (Windgap) Eddie Keher (The Rower-Inistioge).

Subs: PJ Ryan (The Fenians), Brian Cody (James Stephens), Nicky Brennan (Conahy

Shamrocks), Jim Murphy (The Rower-Inistioge), Billy Harte (Galmoy), Shem Delaney (The Fenians), Ger Fennelly (Ballyhale Shamrocks), Dick McNamara (St Senans).

1975
September 7
Kilkenny 2-22 Galway 2-10
Croke Park
Attendance 63,711

Kilkenny: Noel Skehan (Bennettsbridge), Fan Larkin (James Stephens), Nicky Orr (The Fenians), Brian Cody (James Stephens), Pat Lawlor (Bennettsbridge), Pat Henderson (The Fenians), Tom McCormack (James Stephens), Liam 'Chunky' O'Brien (James Stephens), Frank Cummins (Blackrock, Cork), Mick Crotty (James Stephens), Pat Delaney (The Fenians), Billy Fitzpatrick (The Fenians), captain, Mick 'Cloney' Brennan (Erin's Own), Kieran Purcell (Windgap), Eddie Keher (The Rower- Inistioge).

Subs: PJ Ryan (The Fenians), Ger Fennelly (Ballyhale Shamrocks), Nicky Brennan (Conahy Shamrocks), Jim Treacy (Bennettsbridge), Ger Henderson (The Fenians), Matt Ruth (St Patrick's, Ballyraggett).

Prendergast

When Kilkenny retained the Leinster title in 1987, Clara's Paddy Prendergast captained the team from the full-back position, though disappointment awaited in a mean-spirited All-ireland final against Galway.

chapter 10

PADDY PRENDERGAST

1979

"I played my underage hurling with Clara, St Kieran's and the Kilkenny minors almost exclusively at centre back. Curiously, I never played there in the senior inter-county Championship, spending time alternating between the full-back line and left half-back. My adult days with my club were also as a full-back.

I found playing at wing-back extremely enjoyable. The play was more open and it was possible to influence a game more from that position than from full-back. Sometimes the flow of the game would enable you to play loosely, while, in others, your target was, perhaps, to cancel out the opposition's best forward. That the role changed from day-to-day made it challenging.

Full-back play was more restricted. You were always conscious that a simple mistake, or an unlucky bounce of the ball, could turn a game. The position was not unlike that of a goalkeeper in that there was rarely a second chance to recover from a mistake or a bit of bad luck, as, by then, the ball could be resting in your net.

Following our All-Ireland wins in 1982 and 1983, Kilkenny were expected to make a strong bid for the 1984 Centenary final. Ultimately, the year turned into a disaster, both for Kilkenny, who lost the Leinster semi-final to Wexford, and for me as I had fractured my leg in the quarter final. Such is sport.

Losing the 1987 All-Ireland final as captain was a huge disappointment. While Galway were the better team on the day, there was something lacking in our approach that wrecked our chances. That game turned out to be my last inter-county

Championship game as I was on the subs' bench for the 1988 Leinster semi-final defeat by Wexford. I subsequently retired at the commencement of the 1988-89 National League.

Championship places on any Kilkenny team are hard-earned and harder still to hold on to. I suppose to have played senior inter-county Championship hurling in four separate defensive positions is a pleasant memory. It certainly compensates for some of the disappointments."

Paddy Prendergast

—⟋⟍—

If pressed to nominate a player who has successfully graduated with distinction through the various academies that constitute Kilkenny hurling, Paddy Prendergast would be such a player. From Clara's Under-12s to All-Ireland senior finals, Paddy passed with distinction all the examinations placed before him. Between the book-ends of his career he became a serial Championship winner at all levels of club, colleges and inter-county hurling.

Paddy was born on February 8, 1958. Almost from the time he began playing competitively he experienced winning ways. He won county titles in 1970 (U-12), 1972 (U-14) and 1974 (minor). He had an opportunity to win a second minor title in 1976, but Clara were defeated by Ballyhale Shamrocks in the county final.

At St Kieran's College, Paddy won two juvenile, three junior and two senior provincial titles, rounding off a spectacular second-level career with a senior All-Ireland medal in 1975 when the competition was run on a 13-a-side formula.

Paddy effortlessly graduated into the inter-county minor scene, winning Leinster and All-Ireland medals in 1975, playing at full-back. The following year, occupying the centre-back slot, he had to be content with a provincial title only as Kilkenny were defeated by Tipperary in the All-Ireland final.

With such dominance of Leinster underage hurling by Kilkenny teams and colleges at the time it was somewhat surprising that only one provincial U-21 title was won. That sole 1977 success was later embellished by an All-Ireland title win when Kilkenny defeated a highly fancied Cork in the final, with

Paddy manning the left corner-back position. He completed a successful year by winning his first adult county title in Clara's county junior Championship win, the club's second title in that grade.

With his career clearly on an upward curve, Paddy's call-up to the county senior team was inevitable. He made his Championship debut at right-corner-back in Kilkenny's 1978 Leinster semi-final win over Offaly, winning his first senior provincial title some weeks later when Wexford were defeated. Having disposed of Galway in the All-Ireland semi-final, Kilkenny faced a daunting task in the final, a Cork side in pursuit of a three-in-a-row. Following a fiercely contested, but unspectacular game, a late goal swung the game Cork's way. While Paddy's debut season in senior ranks ended in acute disappointment, it would not be long before that loss would be made up.

In the course of Kilkenny's defeat of Wexford in the 1979 Leinster final, the selectors were forced to switch Paddy from left corner-back to full-back to arrest developing goalmouth difficulties. With the move paying off Kilkenny regained the momentum to edge clear in the final minutes. Paddy retained the full-back position for the All-Ireland clash with Galway, who had sensationally dented Cork's historic four-in-a-row ambitions in the semi-final. Heavy rain and strong winds over the weekend and on the morning of the game kept the attendance down to 53,535, the lowest since the 1958 final. With the benefit of two somewhat fortuitous goals, one in each half, Kilkenny emerged winners by a seven-point margin. Apart from a spell in the third quarter Galway failed to reproduce the spectacular hurling that had derailed Cork. Otherwise the Kilkenny defence were never seriously troubled, with Paddy manning the full-back position confidently and effectively. Curiously, though he became Kilkenny's tenth All-Ireland winning full-back following that win, Paddy would not fill the position again in Championship hurling until 1986.

In July, 1980, with Paddy an absentee, Kilkenny surrendered their Championship titles to Offaly at a sparsely attended, rain-swept Croke Park. That 3-17 to 5-10 win represented Offaly's first provincial title and was the launching pad towards a spectacularly successful era where eight further provincial titles and four All-Ireland titles were harvested in a style that comprised all that's best in hurling.

Kilkenny's Championship commitments in 1981 were short-lived. A largely experimental   team, with Paddy at right-corner-back, exited the campaign following a Leinster semi-final defeat by Wexford.

At that time Kilkenny's standing in the hurling world was beginning to cause concern, as, in addition to those Championship defeats in 1980 and 1981, Kilkenny had dropped into Division 1(B) of the National League, effectively the League's second division. However, with the appointment of the highly motivated Pat Henderson as sole manager in 1982, the players were not going to be afforded much time or latitude to indulge themselves in their lowly status. Henderson immediately brought to the position the same determination and winning mentality that had exemplified his own successful playing career. Having been one of the most celebrated defenders of his or any other era, Henderson was acutely aware of the necessity of having his backline as near impregnable as possible if his team was to prosper. With Brian Cody, now free of injury, at full-back, and Ger Henderson at centre back, the manager had established the spine of his defence. Paddy was converted into a left half-back, fronting the granite-like figure of the swaggering Dick O'Hara. The right wing of the defence was manned by the combative John Henderson and Nicky Brennan. It was a clear statement by the manager to all other teams that any scores got against his defence would be hard earned.

Promotion out of the National League's lower division was easily secured in the spring of 1982, to be later followed by a win in the League final against Wexford after an absorbing game. The bar had been set. Over the following two years of competition Kilkenny were practically unbeatable, with successive All-Ireland and Leinster titles and a further National League title all added to its inventory. The media, always keen to suitably label unique sporting achievements, duly acknowledged Kilkenny's 'double-double' success. The turnaround in Kilkenny's fortunes were quite remarkable. From 'beaten dockets' of the early years of the decade to serial winners, almost overnight, was an extraordinary achievement, with the two All-Ireland final defeats of Cork being the high points. In each of those finals Paddy had the personal satisfaction of seeing his direct opponents, Tony O'Sullivan and Bertie Og Murphy, both replaced. For his displays throughout 1982, Paddy received an All-Star award. That Kilkenny supplied four other defenders to the 1983 All-Star team militated against him getting a second successive award.

In 1984, Kilkenny were hotly fancied to successfully defend their Championship titles, which achievement would have amounted to a three-in-a-row, a distinction that had tantalised several Kilkenny teams since 1913 but was never achieved. Qualification for the unique and symbolic Centenary Final was also appealing. However, the team's eventual fall was as dramatic as its ascent. An unexpected defeat by Wexford in the Leinster semi-final ensued, a game which Paddy missed having suffered a serious leg injury in the quarter-final. With full-back Brian Cody also an absentee through injury Kilkenny's weakened defence fell victims to a late Tony Doran goal and a three-point defeat, 3-10 to 1-13.

That defeat was followed by a similar setback by Offaly in 1985, after a replay, with Paddy lining out at left half-back. He, with Ger and John Henderson were the only remaining defenders from the 1982-1983 team still on active duty. Dick O'Hara had suffered an eye injury that forced him out of inter-county hurling, while, inexplicably, Brian Cody, Frank Cummins, Billy Fitzpatrick and Nickey Brennan were all substitutes; Noel Skehan had retired, his place going to Championship debutant, David Burke from Urlingford.

Kilkenny, as is their tradition, regrouped. With Paddy now back in the right full-back position, the Leinster title was regained in 1986, but Kilkenny then allowed themselves to be out-thought and out-fought by Galway in the All-Ireland semi-final, losing by 11 points (4-12 to 0-13). The Kilkenny management subsequently came in for severe criticism for their failure to counteract Galway's three-man midfield and two-man full-forward line formation, a tactic which effectively won them the game.

When Kilkenny retained the Leinster title in 1987 Paddy captained the team from the full-back position. In a somewhat mean-spirited, dour game, Kilkenny lost out to Galway in the All-Ireland final by a six-point margin. Kilkenny's early outfield dominance was generally wasted, leaving them vulnerable to a strong Galway finish. Thus Paddy's relationship with All-Ireland Sunday ended as it began nine years previously, with a defeat.

Paddy was on the substitute's bench for Kilkenny Leinster semi-final defeat by Wexford in 1988, the last time his name appeared on a Championship panel.

Paddy's captaincy of the team in 1987 arose by virtue of Clara's last-gasp win over Ballyhale Shamrocks in the 1986 county senior final. Having won the intermediate county title in 1982 the senior grade had proved somewhat difficult for Clara, their best year being 1983 when they reached the semi-final. Sadly, the team did not develop as expected, following that 1986 win, qualifying for only one other county final, 1990, where they were convincingly defeated by Glenmore.

At representative level, Paddy was honoured by the Leinster selectors for two inter-provincial campaigns. He was a substitute on the successful 1979 team and was full-back on the 1987 team that lost to Connacht in the final.

In 1984, Kilkenny won its first Oireachtas Tournament since 1969, giving Paddy his sole win in that competition. He won his only Walsh Cup medal in 1988.

Paddy's hurling talents have been inherited by his three sons, David, Shane and Niall. They each hold All-Ireland Senior Colleges medals and numerous provincial titles at juvenile, junior and senior levels with St Kieran's College. Shane and David have each won Intermediate All-Ireland titles, while all three have won both Minor and U-21 All-Ireland titles.

In August, 2003, the Prendergast families, and the wider Clara community, suffered the untimely death from cancer of Paddy's half-brother, Anthony Prendergast. Anthony was a gifted hurler and played a key role in all Clara's major wins, especially the 1986 senior county final. He represented Kilkenny at all grades from U-14 to senior, winning All-Ireland medals, at U-21 in 1984 and senior in 1993.

Paddy, who farms with his wife, Margaret, at Higginstown, Clara, experienced a tremendously rewarding career. From his successful club days to his fruitful St Kieran's College days, right through to becoming an inter-county All-Ireland medallist in three separate grades, he was a winner on all fronts. He played senior inter-county Championship hurling in four defensive positions, performing magnificently in each. Possessing all the basic skills in abundance, Paddy was also endowed with that extra essential mix of determination and competitive zeal that are the calling cards of all special players, of which he was unquestionably one. Following their second successive All-Ireland final defeat by Kilkenny in 1983, a well-known Cork County Board delegate and a former All-Ireland winner remarked: "We will remain in the hurling backwater unless and until we can unearth a few defenders who can play with the frightening determination and fearless commitment that Paddy Prendergast displays with Kilkenny." Clearly, that Corkman knew his hurling.

CAREER HIGHLIGHTS

All-Ireland senior finalist: 1978, 1979, 1982, 1983 and 1987

All-Ireland senior winner: 1979, 1982 and 1983

Leinster senior winner: 1978, 1979, 1982, 1983, 1986 and 1987

All-Ireland U-21 winner: 1977

Leinster U-21 winner: 1977

All-Ireland minor winner: 1975

Leinster minor winner: 1975 and 1976

National League winner: 1981–82, 1982–83 and 1985–86

Railway Cup winner: 1979

Oireachtas Tournament winner: 1984

Walsh Cup winner: 1988

All-Star award: 1982

County senior winner: 1986

County intermediate winner: 1982

County junior winner: 1977

County U-21 winner: 1979

County minor winner: 1974 (with Clara Bennettsbridge)

County U-14 winner: 1972

County U-12 winner: 1970

All-Ireland senior colleges winner: 1975

Leinster colleges winner: 7 (two juvenile, three junior and two senior)

ALL-IRELAND WINNING TEAM
1979
September 2
Kilkenny 2-12 Galway 1-8
Croke Park
Attendance 53,535

Kilkenny: Noel Skehan (Bennettsbridge), Fan Larkin (James Stephens), Paddy Prendergast (Clara) John Henderson (The Fenians), Richie Reid (Ballyhale Shamrocks), Ger Henderson (The Fenians), Nicky Brennan (Conahy Shamrocks), Joe Hennessy (James Stephen's) Frank Cummins (Blackrock, Cork), Ger Fennelly (Ballyhale Shamrocks) captain, Billy Fitzpatrick (The Fenians), Liam 'Chunky' O'Brien (James Stephens), Mick 'Cloney' Brennan (Erin's Own), Mick Crotty (James Stephens), Matt Ruth (St Patrick's, Ballyraggett).

Subs: Maurice Mason (Ballyhale Shamrocks), Billy Walton (James Stephens), Murty Kennedy (St Lachtain's), Kevin Fennelly (Ballyhale Shamrocks), replaced Crotty, (injured 51 mins; Tommy Malone (The Rower-Inistioge) John Marnell (Dicksboro).

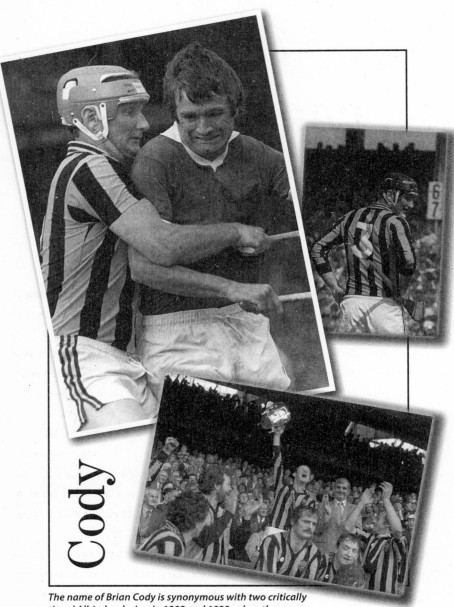

Cody

The name of Brian Cody is synonymous with two critically timed All-Ireland wins, in 1982 and 1983, when the legend from James Stephens produced memorable repeat performances with his mastery of two Cork icons, Ray Cummins and Jimmy Barry-Murphy.

chapter 11

"Playing with Kilkenny was a tremendous honour, but it was also a serious responsibility. You had made the panel, you had trained hard with a certain target in mind – to win and to play well if you were selected were the priorities. Match day was not a day to be burdening yourself with extra baggage like the historical significance of what you may or may not be about to achieve. The opposition, and your immediate opponent, were enough to keep you focused. If you did not give them the respect they were they were due you could be in for a tough afternoon. And a short career.

Despite all the memorable days that I have experienced with Kilkenny, both as a player and manager, it was two wins by my club that gave me the most satisfaction. Those wins, the County final in 2004 and the All-Ireland Club final in 2005, were, to me, what the essence of the GAA is about. Club success and achievement mean everything to me. The club made me as a hurling person, and in many other ways as well.

I could never understand county players not putting in the maximum effort on behalf of their clubs. These players owe a lot to their clubs, and the clubs, in turn, need them to perform at the best of their abilities on a consistent level. Not only am I happy as a manager that these players return to club action as committed and determined as possible, but I also encourage it.

As a manager I have never had any difficulty accommodating Third Level coaches with priority use of county players for their competitions. The Fitzgibbon Cup, for example, is a terrific platform for any player with ambitions. The standard of play is consistently of a very high order while, in a lot of cases, it's the players themselves who are coaching their teams, together with organising the matches. What better experiences could they accumulate? When these players became available to you they were very well grounded in many facets of the game. You knew instantly that they were serious about their game.

Also, in many situations it's the player's first experience of playing in unfamiliar surroundings, away from the comfort of their family-orientated clubs. I have no doubt that players such as Henry Shefflin, JJ Delaney, Jackie Tyrell, John Tennyson and Michael Rice, to mention just a few, benefited enormously from their Fitzgibbon Cup days."

Brian Cody

—⟡—

To suggest that the career of a player who won senior, club, U-21, minor and colleges All-Ireland medals has almost become overshadowed by his subsequent managerial career might appear somewhat eccentric, to say the least. Yet that is what has almost happened in the case of Brian Cody. By the way, the inclusion of the adverb in the above two sentences is deliberate. To the more seasoned generation of Kilkenny supporter, the name Brian Cody is synonymous with two critically timed All-Ireland wins in 1982 and 1983, with his All-Ireland win of 1975 merely "taken into consideration". In those wins of the 1980s Brian produced memorable repeat performances of how to make difficult assignments look relatively easy where his mastery of two Cork icons, Ray Cummins and Jimmy Barry-Murphy were crucial elements in Kilkenny's wins. To that generation of supporters Brian's subsequent managerial successes were no more than what was to be expected

—⟡—

Yet, to Kilkenny followers of the 25 years and younger age group, the mention of Brian Cody conjures images of momentous September Sundays at Croke Park with the big James Stephens man positioned on the sideline, showing no more emotion than perhaps a brief smile, a clearly unrehearsed jig, or maybe a clenched fist, as another title is added to his beloved county's inventory

As Brian's managerial career is extant, a final audit of his hurling life cannot yet be signed off. Nonetheless, a list his achievements to date does, to say the least, make interesting reading.

Brian was born on the July 12, 1954. Given his family background it was only to be expected that he would find an outlet in hurling. His parents, Bill and Annie (formerly Hoyne) were hurling people whose abiding passion was the development and expansion of Ireland's sporting jewel that is hurling. Bill Cody was one of the driving forces behind the reincarnation of the near moribund James Stephens club in the mid-1960s to become one of the country's most progressive and successful clubs

On commencing playing competitively, Brian very quickly acquired the winning formula, one that has remained with him to date, on either side of the white line. His early successes were in the City U-12 leagues, of which he won two. With St Patrick's, as the juvenile section of James Stephens was known, Brian won successive U-14 county titles in 1966 and 1967. Two U-16 titles followed in 1968 and 1970, together with successive minor titles in 1970 and 1971.

Running in tandem with his club successes Brian experienced an equally bountiful colleges career with St Kieran's College. He was a multiple winner of provincial Championships at juvenile, junior and senior levels. In 1971 he rounded of his second-level hurling education with a senior All-Ireland title win.

Brian experienced two profitable years at minor inter-county level, winning a Leinster title in 1971 and Leinster and All-Ireland titles in 1972. As captain of that team, Brian became the first James Stephens clubman to captain a Kilkenny All-Ireland winning team.

While Brian's tenure at inter-county U-21 level was rewarding, it could have been much more so if bizarre officialdom had not intervened. In 1973, the Central Council decreed that counties could compete at three levels only in the Championships. Kilkenny opted not to compete at U-21 level. Considering that he later played in that year's senior All-Ireland final it is reasonable to assume that Brian would have made the U-21 team had one existed. Nonetheless, Brian departed the U-21 grade with successive Leinster and All-Ireland titles in 1974 and 1975

At club U-21 level, Brian was not so successful. He did win county titles in 1969 and 1970 but subsequently tasted defeat in the finals of 1971, 1972, 1973 and 1974.

While he was learning his craft at minor and U-21 levels, Brian had already begun his senior club career, making his Championship debut in 1971 in the defeat of St Lachtain's. In 1973, he was centre-back on the team that lost one of the most remarkable county finals ever seen at Nowlan Park. Despite leading by 13 points at one stage in the first half, and by 10 points at half time, the Stephens had no answer to a thundering Fenians' fight-back, inspired by Pat Henderson, Pat Delaney and Nicky Orr, which led to a 7-8 to 5-10 win.

Within two years Brian had secured his first senior county title. That win, the club's fourth, was soon embellished with Leinster and All-Ireland honours, the latter achievement followed a memorable win at rain-sodden Thurles, over a Blackrock team infused with a glut of high-profile intercounty players. That win earned James Stephens the distinction of becoming the first Kilkenny club to win the All-Ireland title.

Brian won his second county title the following year, but an unexpected defeat by Laois champions, Camross, deprived James Stephens of the opportunity to replicate the previous year's achievements.

Brian made his Senior inter-county debut in October, 1972, in a National League game against Limerick, some few weeks following his All-Ireland Minor win. He made his senior Championship debut as a replacement in Kilkenny's 2-19 to 2-11 Leinster semi-final win over Dublin in July 1973. Some weeks before Kilkenny faced Limerick in that year's All-Ireland final, Brian's clubmate, and Kilkenny left half-back, Eamonn Morrissey, emigrated to Australia. Brian was selected to fill the vacancy for the final, a game which an injury-ravaged Kilkenny lost decisively. Within 12 months, a full-strength Kilkenny reversed that result but Brian was a substitute on that occasion.

When Kilkenny retained the McCarthy Cup in 1975, Brian was, by then, the team's first choice left corner-back. At the year's end he won his first All-Star award, the citation for which read: "For all his supreme self assurance and the exciting spirit of adventure he has shown at such an early stage of his senior career." With some minor alterations the citation could be used to describe Brian's entire career, both as a player and manager.

Brian won the first of his three National League titles in the final of the 1975–76 competition. That win, and the style with which it was achieved, installed Kilkenny as short odds to retain the All-Ireland title. Before they could gather any momentum in pursuit of the three-in-a-row Kilkenny were demolished by Wexford in the Leinster final, losing by a 17-point margin. That defeat heralded a lean year for Kilkenny as they subsequently lost the finals of the 1976–77 National League and 1977 Leinster Championship.

Due to injury, temporary loss of form and the emergence of future greats – such as Dick O'Hara, Paddy Prendergast, Ger Henderson and Joe Hennessey – Brian was unable to command a place in Kilkenny's defence as the 1978 season swung into action. He was on the substitute's bench when Kilkenny were defeated by Clare in the final of the 1977–78 National League. However, the selectors then saw a role for him in the forward line and it was at full-forward that he played throughout the Championship, which ended in a defeat by Cork in the All-Ireland final. Whether rumours of a less than a favourable reception afforded him on the team's return after that Cork defeat are more than that, Brian did not let the incident, if there was one, affect him at all.

An ankle fracture in the winter of 1978 effectively took Brian out of contention for the 1979 Championship, which Kilkenny subsequently won. He did, however, play for the club in their county semi-final defeat by Erin's Own.

Brian made his Championship debut as a full-back in Kilkenny's Leinster semi-final win over Wexford. Whatever higher ambitions the team had were later quashed in a Croke Park downpour as Offaly out-scored them by 3-17 to 5-10 to win their first provincial title. Clearly not a memorable day for defences.

For the 1981 Leinster semi-final against Wexford, Brian started on the substitute's bench. A new-look defence was in difficulties from the opening minutes, leading to Brian's early introduction. The slide was stopped but not enough to prevent an early exit from the Championship.

In 1982, and now free from injury, Brian was installed at full-back in a defence that, over time, became almost impregnable. The two All-Ireland final wins over Cork were momentous days in the history of Kilkenny hurling. The 1982 win was unexpected, but the ruthlessness, in the sporting sense, by which it was engineered was intoxicating to watch. While the 1983 win was less emphatic, both on the field and scoreboard, it removed any 'once off' tag from the 1982 result. It confirmed once again Kilkenny's propensity to win finals, whatever the odds. In both finals Brian gave masterclass displays of modern full-back play, bringing the rare combination of cool intelligence, strong physical presence and ample hurling skill to an unprecedented level. Sadly, that 1983 final was to prove Brian's last competitive inter-county Championship game

Meanwhile, James Stephens had been overtaken in the late 1970s by Ballyhale Shamrocks as the county's leading club. However, they regrouped and with a new-look team won their sixth county title in 1981, which they followed up with Leinster and All-Ireland honours. That county final win gave Brian the captaincy of Kilkenny for the 1982 successful Championship, an honour which he carried out with distinction.

The recurrence of injury problems took Brian out of consideration for the 1984 Leinster Championship team. His loss was, without question, a contributory factor in Kilkenny's unexpected Leinster semi-final defeat by Wexford.

Brian was in the panel for Kilkenny's defeat by Offaly in the 1985 Leinster semi-final. He did not play any part in that game, one that was to prove his last outing in an inter-county Championship panel. He did continue on to play at club level, his last competitive game for his beloved James Stephens being the 1987 county semi-final defeat by Glenmore.

Though a serial winner of all hurling's honours, Brian rarely won Railway Cup recognition. He came on as a replacement in the 1976 losing final, winning his only interprovincial medal as a substitute in 1977.

When his playing days were over Brian remained involved with St Patrick's National School where he has been based since he qualified as a teacher. He has managed James Stephens for some years without much success in regard to winning a senior title. A defeat by Young Irelands in the replayed 1996 final was the closest he came to ultimate success.

Following the All-Ireland win in 1993, Kilkenny's Championship fortunes dipped dramatically – the next four Leinster titles were shared equally between Offaly and Wexford. Qualifying for the 1998 All-Ireland final failed to galvanise either the team or the followers. The spark that led to the wins of 1982 and 1983 under Pat Henderson, and those of 1992 and 1993 under Ollie Walsh, was missing. A change was needed.

In November, 1998, Brian was appointed manager of the senior team. Though his debut year ended with an agonising one-point defeat in the All-Ireland final, it was evident that, with a little luck, Kilkenny's fortunes were in safe hands. From that defeat Brian later acknowledged that he learned much about himself as a manager and his team, lessons that have been put to profitable use over the last decade. In that time Kilkenny have won nine All-Ireland titles, six National Leagues and have been Leinster champions every year except for 2004 and 2012. Also, under Brian's management, 74 All-Star awards have come to the county, while six of his players, DJ Carey, JJ Delaney, Eoin Larkin, Tommy Walsh, Michael Fennelly and Henry Shefflin (twice) have won The Hurler of The Year awards.

The final few weeks of the 2012 Championship saw Brian display some previously unseen facets to his personality that make him difficult to pigeonhole. He was forceful, direct but not vindictive in his comments on Tipperary's Padraigh Maher's wild stroke on Michael Rice in the All-Ireland semi-final, an injury that caused Rice to miss the remainder of the hurling season, at best.

Brian then made some pre-All-Ireland final comments as to what the role and responsibilities should be of the referee for that game. Comments that were, at best, misunderstood and, at worst, deemed inappropriate. He then refused to get involved in the media-fuelled madness that surrounded Galway's Joe Canning's post-All-Ireland final comments concerning Henry Shefflin's sportsmanship. And, finally, when Brian's team for the All-Ireland final replay was announced, the hurling public in Kilkenny and outside were shocked by some of his selections. However, like most matters concerning Brian and hurling, he was once again proved right as an 11-point win confirms.

Together with Mickey Harte, Brian O'Driscoll, Mick O'Dwyer, Sean Boylan, Paul O'Connell, Padraig Harrington, Sonia O'Sullivan, Katie Taylor and Aidan O'Brien, Brian has become one of the most recognisable faces and voices in Irish sport. He is constantly in demand to address conferences, seminars and such events throughout the country, on both sporting and non-sporting issues. He never disappoints. Brian has been the recipient of every category of award imaginable, probably the most unlikely of which was being awarded RTE's Man of the Match following the 2008 All-Ireland win. He has also been made a Freeman of Kilkenny, the highest civic award available, and one that is sparingly awarded.

Brian's early education and participation in sport was in an era when there was far less knowledge about, and less reliance upon, physical fitness than is presently the case. Yet, he has adapted many of those modern principles and techniques of team preparation and management which, when added to his own beliefs, systems and intelligence, have brought unprecedented success to his teams. Quality rather than quantity time spent on the training field, players' diet control, enlarged panels, the successful development of team spirit that has become unbreakable, elite medical, athletic and physiotherapy back-up, are some examples of the areas where Brian was particularly innovative. He trusts his players implicitly, a trust that is reciprocated without demur.

Being acutely aware of the need to meet the desires and expectations of the local and general hurling public, Brian has insisted that, where possible, all training sessions at Nowlan Park are open affairs. He sees this bond between the players and the public as being a vital cog in the machine that is Kilkenny hurling.

Brian has embraced the creation of the GPA with typical practicality and stoicism. He is on record as stating that he has no problems with much of their work, but lending support to demands, either covert or overt, for pay-for-play is a road he will not be travelling.

Both as a player and as a manager Brian has scaled very lofty heights. Recently retired National Hurling Coaching Director, Paudie Butler, described Brian as 'the master of all time. His equal has not existed'. Surely a fitting tribute to a man who modestly describes himself as 'simply a hurling man'.

One final thought remains: During his underage playing days, Brian won four county U-16 and one Leinster Colleges junior football Championship. Where would Kilkenny hurling be now, had the unthinkable occurred?

CAREER HIGHLIGHTS

All-Ireland senior finalist: 1973, 1974 (s), 1975, 1978, 1982 and 1983

Leinster senior winner: 1973, 1974, 1975, 1978, 1982 and 1983

National League winner: 1975-76, 1981–82 and 1982–83

All-Ireland U-21 winner: 1974 and 1975

Leinster U-21 Winner: 1974 and 1975

All-Ireland minor winner: 1972

Leinster U-21 winner: 1971 and 1972

Railway Cup winner: 1977

All-Star winner: 1975 and 1982

CLUB

All-Ireland senior winner: 1975-76 and 1981-82

Leinster senior wins: 1975-76 and 1981-82

County senior wins: 1975-1976 and 1981

County U-21 wins: 1969 and 1970

County minor wins: 1970 and 1971

County U-16 wins: 1968 and 1970

County U-14 wins: 1966 and 1967

City U-12 League wins: 1965 and 1966

County U-16 football wins: 1967-1970

Dublin U-21 winner: 1974

COLLEGES

Leinster juvenile, junior and senior: 1967-1973

All-Ireland senior winner: 1971

MANAGER

All-Ireland senior wins: 2000, 2002, 2003, 2006, 2007, 2008, 2011, 2012

Leinster senior wins: 1999-2003, 2005-2011

National League wins: 2002, 2003, 2005, 2006, 2009, 2012

ALL-IRELAND WINNING TEAMS

1982
September 5
Kilkenny 3-18 Cork 1-13
Croke Park
Attendance 59,550

Kilkenny: Noel Skehan (Bennetsbridge), John Henderson (The Fenians), Brian Cody (James Stephens) captain, Dick O'Hara (Thomastown United), Nicky Brennan (Conahy Shamrocks), Ger Henderson (The Fenians), Paddy Prendergast (Clara), Joe Hennessy (James Stephens), Frank Cummins (Blackrock, Cork), Richie Power (Carrickshock United), Ger Fennelly (Ballyhale Shamrocks), Kieran Brennan (Conahy Shamrocks), Billy Fitzpatrick (The Fenians), Christy Heffernan (Glenmore) Liam Fennelly, (Ballyhale Shamrocks).

Subs: Kevin Fennelly (Ballyhale Shamrocks), Paddy Neary (James Stephens), Tom McCormack (James Stephens), Matt Ruth (St Patrick's, Ballyraggett), Mick 'Cloney' Brennan (Erin's Own), Billy Purcell (The Fenians) Dinny McCormack (James Stephens), Frank Holohan (Ballyhale Shamrocks), Paudie Lannon (Thomastown United), Eamonn Wallace (Erin's Own), Billy Walton (James Stephens).

1983
September 4
Kilkenny 2-14 Cork 2-12
Attendance 58,381

Kilkenny: Noel Skehan (Bennettsbridge), John Henderson (The Fenians), Brian Cody (James Stephens), Dick O'Hara (Thomastown United), Joe Hennessy (James Stephens), Ger Henderson (The Fenians), Paddy Prendergast (Clara), Frank Cummins (Blackrock, Cork), Ger Fennelly (Ballyhale Shamrocks), Richie Power (Carrickshock United), Kieran Brennan (Conahy Shamrocks), Harry Ryan (Clara), Billy Fitzpatrick (The Fenians), Christy Heffernan (Glenmore), Liam Fennelly, captain, (Ballyhale Shamrocks).

Subs: Kevin Fennelly (Ballyhale Shamrocks), Nicky Brennan (Conahy Shamrocks),

Paddy Neary (James Stephens), Tom McCormack (James Stephens), Sean Fennelly (Ballyhale Shamrocks), Paudie Lannon (Thomastown United), replaced Power, (injured, 69mins); Mickey Kelly (Ballyhale Shamrocks), Billy Purcell (The Fenians), Gordon Ryan (St Lachtain's), Eamonn Wallace (Erin's Own).

Dwyer

Pat Dwyer had a shorter Kilkenny career than some in the full-back line but, having reverted to the last line of defence, he proved his mettle when, in the county's double success in 1992 and '93, The Cats conceded a mere eight goals and 127 points in a 10-game unbeaten run.

chapter 12

"My introduction to inter-county hurling came about through the 1988 junior Championship, which Kilkenny won. I was promoted to the senior team shortly afterwards, making my debut against Antrim in a National League game.

Prior to playing full-back for the senior team I had never previously played there. I had played in the half-back line for my club from my underage days and was centre-back when Kilkenny won that 1988 junior All-Ireland. In my debut game against Antrim I played at left half-back.

When John Henderson retired shortly after the 1991 All-Ireland final defeat a vacancy occurred in the full-back position. Thus, for the 1992 Championship, I was switched to full-back, with Pat O'Neill coming in at centre-back. For the following five Championships I played at full-back.

By the time I moved to full-back, hurling had gone through various changes. In addition to some rule changes, there was now a different approach to collective training. Pre-Championship training was starting earlier each year with the result that with players getting fitter, games became faster and more open. Previously, action around the square tended to be more robust and physical. Now it was more free-flowing and less confrontational. Brian Cody was the perfect example of the new style full-back. My years as a centre-back helped me enormously at full-back, as there was now little difference between the demands of both positions. The requirements to play full-back suited my physique, my style and, I suppose, my temperament.

The early years of the '90s were memorable ones. Our team evolved from a low base and went on to contest three All-Ireland finals, winning two. What makes sport so interesting is that it never stops changing. No sooner had we established ourselves, and expected to develop further, than we were dethroned by Wexford in the 1994 Leinster semi-final. Kilkenny did not win a further Leinster title until 1998, by which time I had retired.

When pursuing your own career you tend not to dwell too much on the achievements of your predecessors, though you are always aware of them and are very proud of them. Even to survive in the game required your fullest attention. You were always aware that, unless you were fully focused in relation to training and matches, your career could be over very quickly. There wasn't much room for side issues."

Pat Dwyer

—ɷɷ—

The All-Ireland junior Championship was introduced in 1912. Kilkenny's success ratio in this competition is far less impressive than in the Association's other flagship grades. Yet, over the years, the senior team has benefited from a regular supply of players who had experienced success of varying degrees at the lower grade. Players such as Jack 'Sag' Carroll (1926), Shem Downey, Pat 'Diamond' Hayden, Mick Kenny, Peter Prendergast and Bill Cahill (1946), John Sutton, Tom Walsh, Dick Rockett, and Johnny McGovern (1951), Ollie Walsh, Tom Walsh (for the second time), Jim 'Link' Walsh, Denis Heaslip, Billie Dwyer and Mick Fleming (1957), Michael Walsh, John Power and Liam McCarthy (1986), Liam Simpson (1990), James McGarry and Eamonn Kennedy (1995) were all Championship winners at junior level before repeating those success at the higher grade.

Omitted from the above list is Pat Dwyer, a player who featured on the successful 1988 junior team and who later progressed to the senior team where he became the anchor man in a team that contested three consecutive All-Ireland finals. Pat, a farmer from Croan, in the parish of Aghaviller, became Kilkenny's 12th All-Ireland winning full-back in a career that was extraordinary successful, despite being relatively short in comparison to those of some of his full-back associates.

Pat was born on December 19th, 1965, into a farming family. He duly attended Newmarket National School. His underage days were barren ones as regards winning titles, and it was not until 1986, when Carrickshock United won the Rionn B U-21 county title, that he won his first Championship medal. His other club successes came, first in 1998 when the South junior title was won, and, second, in 1999 when Intermediate status was attained following the club's 1-6 to 0-8 win over Emeralds in the county final. That win gave Pat his sole adult county Championship honour.

Curiously, Pat failed to attract the attention of a succession of county minor and U-21 selection committees. In 1988, however, his quality performances with his club were rewarded when county junior manager, Ollie Walsh, came calling. Pat rewarded his manager's faith in him by playing a pivotal role from the centre-back position in Kilkenny's march to Leinster and All-Ireland honours. Pat and his manager would share further All-Ireland highs and lows in the early years of the fast-approaching 1990s.

Following that junior win, Pat was immediately promoted to the senior team, seeing National League action over the winter of 1988/89. He made his Championship debut in the 1989 Leinster quarter final win over Westmeath, playing at full-back. He held the position for Kilkenny's two other Championship games that year, the semi-final win over Wexford and the final defeat by Offaly.

Pat was subsequently switched to centre-back for the 1989/90 National League campaign, which Kilkenny won, defeating Wexford in the 'home' final and New York in the final proper. In the subsequent Leinster semi-final, Kilkenny left all previous good form behind them and were totally routed by an outstanding Offaly side on a 4-15 to 1-9 scoreline.

Still playing at centre-back, Pat won his first Leinster senior title in July, 1991, following Kilkenny's two-point win over Dublin. Some weeks later he endured the bitter disappointment of narrowly losing the All-Ireland final to Tipperary. To add to Pat's woes was the stark realisation that the game was one that Kilkenny should have won. Failure to turn near total first-half dominance to their advantage left them exposed to a late, decidedly freakish Tipperary goal and ultimate defeat. Following the game Kilkenny manager Ollie Walsh remarked that he had learned valuable lessons from the defeat, ones that would be put to good use in the future. He practically guaranteed Kilkenny followers a victory if a further opportunity to win an All-Ireland title was afforded him. How prescient he proved to be.

Changes were made to the team for the 1992 Championship, the most far reaching being the restoration of Pat to the full-back position and the recall of Willie O'Connor and Pat O'Neill as first-choice selections in the respective left half-back and centre-back positions. With largely unaltered teams Kilkenny won the 1992 and 1993 Championships, overcoming Cork and Galway respectively in the finals. A feature of that double success was the miserliness of the team's defence, which conceded a mere 8 goals and 127 points in its ten-game unbeaten run, while the various Kilkenny attacking units accounted for 27 goals and 144 points.

All through both successful campaigns Pat was the essence of cool, calculating defending. He held a variety of opponents scoreless, and, in the process, conceded neither frees nor influence to any of them. In the 1993, his starting opponent, Joe Rabbitte, is credited with scoring four points, all of which were scored after he switched positions. Clearly, strong, disciplined defending on the edge of the Kilkenny square is not exclusively a modern invention. That Pat was awarded an All-Star for 1992 only is another example of the multitude of unfathomable selections made by the All-Star selectors over the years, ones that have, from time to time, shaken the credibility of the entire awards system.

Following their exertions in reaching three successive Championship finals, it was no real surprise that Kilkenny's attempts at reaching a fourth came unstuck in the 1994 Leinster semi-final against Offaly. The midland outfit had regrouped during Kilkenny's provincial dominance of the previous three years, and, with some of the most skilful hurlers of any era playing the purest hurling imaginable, they comfortably divested Kilkenny of their hard-fought titles, which they themselves then accumulated with typical style.

An impressive 1994/95 National League campaign, embellished with a clear-cut win against Clare in the final, seemed to indicate that Kilkenny's lethargy of 1994 was a mere aberration. Leinster followers eagerly awaited the next Championship clash between the reigning league and Championship title holders. It came in the Leinster final, but was one which turned out a total mismatch. Offaly swept Kilkenny aside with a brand of hurling that was once a Kilkenny trademark to register a win that was, in all probability, their most treasured. They made light of the continuous downpour to put on a hurling exhibition to which Kilkenny simply had no answer. Were it not for two late DJ Carey goals, Kilkenny's losing margin would most certainly have reached embarrassing proportions.

That 1995 defeat practically heralded the beginning of the end of that Kilkenny team, their demise as serious contenders was confirmed by their 1996 Leinster quarter-final defeat by Wexford. Ollie Walsh later retired as manager and Pat would not represent his county again in Championship hurling.

Pat resides at Croan with his wife, Pauline and son Edward, won two Walsh Cup medals, 1989 and 1992. He represented Leinster in the inter provincial Championships but failed to win a coveted Railway Cup medal.

While Kilkenny's Championship win in 1993 was not as emotionally charged as that of 1992, what it did confirm was Pat's place in the inventory of eminent Kilkenny full-backs. The rule changes that had been incrementally introduced to hurling over the years were particularly relevant to full-backs. The responsibilities and duties of full-backs, and the manner by which they could be carried out, were seriously altered. If Brian Cody was the trailblazer of the modern full-back, Pat was the finished product. Full-backs now required an armoury of both hurling and athletic skills to survive. With post-match media analysis becoming more forensic and detailed with each passing year, full-backs, probably for the first time ever in the game, were required to be always above reproach. Behind-the-goal cameras did not allow for slippage, either accidental or otherwise. Being tall, agile and deceptively strong, and possessing an abundance of hurling skills, allied to an ice-cool temperament, Pat was the classic template of the new species of full-back. He excelled under the new rules. His lengthy, thoughtful, accurate deliveries out of defence became a feature of his game, He was equally comfortable with both the high and ground ball and, being blessed with an utterly dependable array of flicks and clever touches, he rarely appeared under pressure. In what may appear as a contradiction in terms, Pat appeared to bring a sense of serenity and tranquillity to full-back play.

As noted, Pat experienced a relatively short senior inter-county career. He was, largely, a private man who rarely sought the limelight. His dependability was almost taken for granted by Kilkenny followers. In a perverse, but not in a belittling, way it appears that his greatness was not fully appreciated until a custom-made replacement was required. Such was the standard that Pat set that it was not until the arrival in 2000 of his farming neighbour, 19-year-old Noel Hickey, that it could safely be said that Pat had been adequately replaced.

CAREER HIGHLIGHTS

All-Ireland senior finalist: 1991, 1992 and 1993
All-Ireland senior winner: 1992 and 1993
Leinster senior winner: 1991, 1992 and 1993
All-Ireland junior winner: 1988
Leinster junior winner: 1988
National League winner: 1989/90 and 1994/95
Walsh Cup winner: 1989 and 1992
All-Star award: 1992
Kilkenny U-21 winner: 1986
Kilkenny junior winner: 1999
South junior winner: 1989 and 1999

ALL-IRELAND WINNING TEAMS

1992

September 6

Kilkenny 3-10 Cork 1-12

Croke Park

Attendance 64,354

Kilkenny: Michael Walsh (Dicksboro), Eddie O'Connor (Glenmore), Pat Dwyer (Carrickshock United), Liam Simpson (Bennettsbridge), Liam Walsh (Glenmore), Pat O'Neill (Young Irelands), Willie O'Connor (Glenmore), Michael 'Titch' Phelan (Glenmore), Bill Hennessy (Tullaroan), Liam McCarthy (Piltown), John Power (John Lockes), DJ Carey (Young Irelands), Eamonn Morrissey (St Martin's), Liam Fennelly

(Ballyhale Shamrocks), captain, James 'Shiner' Brennan (Erin's Own).

Subs: Adrian Ronan (Graigue-Ballycallan), replaced Morrissey, 58 mins; Paul Phelan (Ballyhale Shamrocks), Christy Heffernan (Glenmore), replaced Brennan, injured ht; Richie Power (Carrickshock United), Dermot Lawler (St Martin's), Tom Murphy (Mooncoin), Joe Walsh (Mullinavat), Michael Morrissey (Cuala, Dublin), Charlie Carter (Young Irelands).

1993

September 5

Kilkenny 2-17 Galway 1-13

Croke Park

Attendance 63,460

Kilkenny: Michael Walsh (Dicksboro), Eddie O'Connor (Glenmore), captain, Pat Dwyer (Carrickshock United), Liam Simpson (Bennettsbridge), Liam Keoghan (Tullaroan), Pat O'Neill (Young Irelands), Willie O'Connor (Glenmore), Bill Hennessy (Tullaroan), Michael 'Titch' Phelan (Glenmore), Liam McCarthy (Piltown), John Power (John Lockes), D J Carey (Young Irelands), Eamonn Morrissey (St Martin's), P J Delaney (The Fenians), Adrian Ronan (Graigue-Ballycallan).

Subs: Joe Walsh (Mullinavat), Tom Murphy (Mooncoin), (replaced Phelan, 69 mins); Paul Phelan (Ballyhale Shamrocks), James 'Shiner' Brennan (Erin's Own), replaced Morrissey, 59 mins; Anthony Prendergast (Clara), Christy Heffernan (Glenmore), replaced Delaney, injury time; Dermot Lawler (St Martin's), Eamonn Holland (Erin's Own), Brian Ryan (The Fenians).

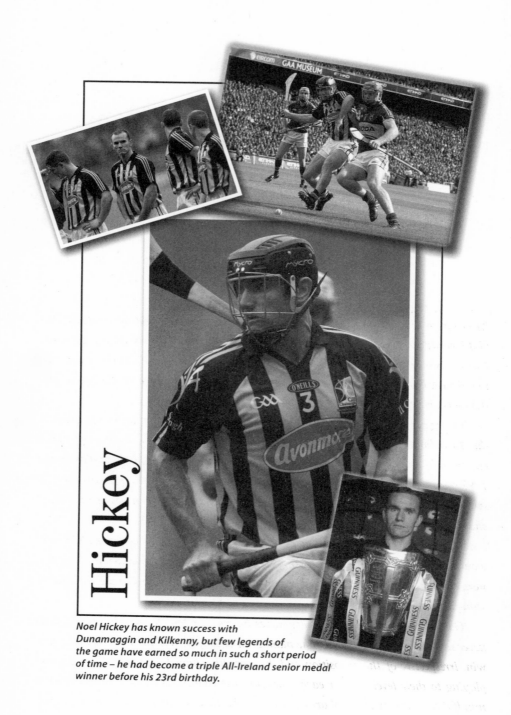

Hickey

Noel Hickey has known success with
Dunamaggin and Kilkenny, but few legends of
the game have earned so much in such a short period
of time – he had become a triple All-Ireland senior medal
winner before his 23rd birthday.

chapter 13

"Apart from my school hurling days, and up to U-16 where I sometimes played in the half-forward line, I have always played in one or other of the full-back line positions. I was, however, once picked centre-forward for a minor county final, but was switched to full-back line just prior to the game. The selectors obviously, and wisely, had second thoughts about their original decision.

Having played in the All-Ireland minor final in 1998, and captained the U-21s to the All-Ireland title in 1999 from full-back I suppose that was the position to which various selection committees thought I was best suited. Being selected to play in the 1997 county senior final was a major boost to my confidence. Though it was my first senior Championship game, that I had my brothers Jim and Tom beside me helped enormously.

Within months of making my senior inter-county Championship debut, Kilkenny won the All-Ireland title. Any notions that there were any guarantees in the game were quickly dispelled the following year when Galway overran us in the All-Ireland semi-final.

Though Kilkenny have been very successful over the last decade, the players have never taken success for granted. The management simply would not tolerate it. Every win, irrespective of the opposition and the score line, have been the result of players playing to their level best for each other and the county. Each and every player is mindful that any displays of arrogance or over-confidence that would lead to a drop in performance would quickly lead to the management finding other players with the proper attitude.

I feel very privileged to be part of this Kilkenny set-up. From Brian Cody down, there is a tremendous sense of ambition and unity within the squad. You learn to put up with the injuries, illness and the defeats and move on to the next target. There is always the next game. Hopefully, that will continue.

As a youngster growing up in Dunamaggin, I was always aware of Jim 'Link' Walshe's achievements with Kilkenny. Sadly, I never spoke to him personally, but I would see him frequently as his farm was close to ours. He and his brother, Tom, another All-Ireland senior winner, were very popular in the parish."

Noel Hickey

—⁓—

County final Sunday 1997 was a historic day the Dunamaggin club, and an auspicious occasion in the advancement of Kilkenny hurling. That day Dunamaggin won its first, and, to date, only senior title while, from the Kilkenny aspect, it heralded the arrival on the adult hurling scene of Noel Hickey.

Dunamaggin had entered the county final as rank outsiders to the DJ Carey led Young Irelands. It was a novel final in that both finalists were relatively new to the senior grade, Young Irelands, having attained senior status in 1992 while Dunamaggin secured similar ranking three years later. Despite their relative inexperience in the premier grade, Young Irelands, with DJ in irrepressible form, won their first senior title in 1996, defeating James Stephens, following a replay.

While Dunamaggin were regarded as a club with great potential, it was felt that they then lacked the overall class and quality to dethrone the champions. The selection of a largely unknown corner-back, yet to reach his 17th birthday, was seen as the ultimate gamble by their selectors, and seemed to confirm to neutrals that the club simply did not have the strength in dept at this stage of their development to win the title. While the player in question, Noel Hickey, had won a Leinster minor medal earlier that year, he had yet to play senior Championship hurling for the club. To launch a player of such tender years, and with such limited experience, in a senior final against an attack that included

DJ Carey and Charlie Carter appeared at best reckless. Yet, at the conclusion of an enthralling game, Dunamaggin emerged victorious and Noel had secured his county senior medal. He was, in all probability, the youngest player to do so in the 100-year plus history of the Championship. However, it was clear to all who witnessed Noel in action that day that Kilkenny had, once again, unearthed a player of rare quality, one who would seamlessly progress to the game's highest levels. He appeared to possess all the essentials in abundance.

One of eight children of Andy and Annie Hickey a farming family from Danganmore, Dunamaggin, Noel was born on December 22nd, 1980. His received his formal education at St Leonard's National School, Dunamaggin, Colaiste Eamon Ris, Callan, and Kildalton Agricultural College, Piltown.

Noel developed the winning formula at an early age. Though only in his tenth year, he won an U-13 Schools' title in 1990. One year later Noel was back on the winner's rostrum, winning a second U-13 county title. He collected his third underage county championship in 1993 when the club won the county U-16 Championship. It was becoming evident that, though a small rural club, Dunamaggin were developing an enviable habit of winning underage championships, and that the seeds for future adult success were being studiously sown.

The year 1995 was a very successful one for the club. The county intermediate, U-21 and minor Championships were all garnered, the wins acknowledging the previous hard work undertaken by the club at underage. The U-21 title was retained in 1996 with the minors narrowly losing the county final and the seniors running eventual champions, Young Irelands, very close in the county semi-final. In hindsight, and on closer examination of the club's attention to underage development, perhaps that senior success in 1997 was not the major surprise it was generally rated to be.

Noel won his second provincial minor medal in 1998, but All-Ireland success eluded him in the defeat by Cork in the final. Earlier that year he won a Leinster Senior Colleges 'A' title with Colaiste Eamonn Ris, Callan, but a two-point, semi-final defeat by St Flannan's College, Ennis, dashed All-Ireland title aspirations.

However, the year ended on a positive note as Dunamaggin won the county U-21 title, their third in four years. That win gave the club the honour of providing the captain for the county U-21 team for 1999. The task fell to Noel, one he dutifully carried out with distinction, leading Kilkenny to its seventh All-Ireland title. Earlier that year he won an Agricultural Colleges All-Ireland Senior title with Kildalton College.

Such was the reputation Noel had now etched for himself that it was a mere question of time before the county senior selectors came calling. The mid- to late 1990s were barren years for the senior team, with qualification for, but subsequent defeats, in the All-Ireland finals of 1998 and 1999 not helping to lift morale. One of the more significant additions that manager Brian Cody made to the panel as he attempted to apply much-needed surgery to the team for the commencement of the 2000 Championship was Noel, who made his debut in the 2000 Leinster semi-final defeat of Dublin, playing at left corner-back. For the remainder of the campaign Noel, featured at full-back.

With wins over Offaly and Galway, Kilkenny were back in the final against their Leinster final victims, Offaly. Under severe pressure not to earn the toxic distinction of being the first Kilkenny team to lose three consecutive finals in as many years, the team made an explosive start and were leading by 2-2 to 0-1 after ten minutes. Keeping up the relentless pressure, and scoring the majority of their chances, Kilkenny won their 26th title by a margin of 13 points. With this victory Noel became Kilkenny's 13th All-Ireland winning full-back, completing the year with his first All-Star award and being named Young Hurler of the Year.

Kilkenny comfortably retained their provincial title in 2001 but came badly unstuck in the semi-final against a hard-pulling, no-frills Galway side. That defeat raised many questions amongst followers as to the state of readiness of both the team and the management for that Galway challenge. Brian Cody would later coldly and clinically assess the reasons for that defeat, address them, and vowed that, if Kilkenny were to be defeated again under his watch, it would be for no other reason than that they had met a superior team.

The following two years saw Kilkenny dominate the game in a manner not seen since their predecessors of the 1982–1983 era. Two All-Ireland senior, two Leinster senior and two National League titles were all hoovered up with a fusion of style, teamwork, determination, fearless defending, imaginative forward play and disciplined ruthlessness. Noel was the essence of Kilkenny's approach throughout that winning run. He had become a triple All-Ireland senior medal winner before his 23rd birthday.

In 2004, Noel endured the contrasting side of sport as Kilkenny surrendered both their hard-won Championship titles to Wexford and Cork, respectively. Surprisingly, that latter defeat, in the All-Ireland final, raised doubts in some circles as to Noel's long-term future as the team's first choice full-back as his direct opponent, Brian Corcoran, proved more than a handful for him. In time Noel would more than balance the books in his duel with Corcoran. His ability to avenge, with profit, previous uncomfortable outings was to prove one of the hallmarks of his career.

By the middle of the 2005 season, both Noel and Kilkenny appeared to have put the travails of the previous year, whether real or imagined, behind them. The National League and the Leinster titles had been regained comfortably, with a return to Croke Park on All-Ireland Sunday looking more than a possibility. However, within a matter of a few weeks, both Noel's and Kilkenny's aspirations were summarily dashed. Noel contracted a cardiac-related virus that forced him to withdraw from the panel prior to the quarter-final game against Limerick. Kilkenny stumbled over the line in that game but, despite scoring 4-18, subsequently lost out to Galway in the semi-final. It is difficult to envisage that, had Noel been in the full-back position, Kilkenny's very creditable tally would not have been sufficient to win the game.

The following three years in Noel's hurling life were years of unbounded accomplishment. He began the 2006 Championship at Leinster final stage playing at left corner-back. Injury and illness had taken him out of the successful National League campaign and the provincial semi-final. He was restored to full-back for the remainder of the campaign. His role in the All-Ireland final win over Cork cannot be overstated, with his mastery over Brian Corcoran a very crucial factor. It was arguably his best-ever performance. He banished the few ghosts that may have been loitering from his 2004 encounter with Corcoran.

In 2007, Noel played throughout all Kilkenny's Championship games leading to the All-Ireland final against Limerick. However, due to a recurrence of a hamstring injury, he was forced out of that game after 25 minutes. Before his enforced departure he had played with the same authority and effectiveness as he had demonstrated in the 2006 final. Such was the extent of the surgery subsequently undertaken by him, and the prolonged period of recuperation, that he played no part in Kilkenny's 2008 National League and provincial Championship wins. That he was able to return and play so brilliantly in the defeat of Cork in the All-Ireland semi-final was nothing short of miraculous. He was largely untroubled in the subsequent demolition of Waterford in the All-Ireland final.

Further injury problems hampered Noel's attempts to reclaim his place on the team for the start of the 2009 season. He saw no action in Kilkenny's League-Championship double success, despite his heroic attempts to regain his place. The management team felt that he simply did not have enough competitive hurling behind him to warrant selection on the team for the All-Ireland final, despite a growing public demand for his inclusion. If ever a player deserved to have played in that historic four-in-a row win it was Noel, but fate decreed otherwise.

Following quality performances in the latter stages of the 2010 National League, Noel was recalled for the Championship campaign, which concluded with a comprehensive defeat in the All-Ireland final. The extent and nature of Kilkenny's defeat raised the debate as to the long-term future of many of their long-serving players, including Noel. There is no doubt but that the Kilkenny's defence eventually wilted against the relentless Tipperary pressure, but the problems were due to combined defensive frailties, rather than of any particular player not performing. The plague of injuries that robbed Kilkenny of the services of Brian Hogan for the entire game, that of Henry Shefflin's, bar the opening quarter, and limited the effectiveness of Tommy Walsh and John Tennyson throughout, were as significant factors in Kilkenny's defeat as was Tipperary's impressive performance.

The hurling media, the majority of outside hurling followers, and a large proportion of Kilkenny supporters, confidently predicted that, following that Tipperary defeat, Noel's days as a Kilkenny defender were behind him. Such public pessimism as to his worth makes his achievements throughout 2011 all the more remarkable. Such was his determination to succeed that he personally had no self doubts. He played in some of Kilkenny's National League and Walsh Cup games, alternating between full-back and corner-back.

He survived Kilkenny's demolition by Dublin in the National League final and began the Leinster Championship at right corner-back. It appeared as if even the management were also unsure of his ability to again hold down his favourite No.3 position. He was, however, restored to the full-back position for the Leinster final against Dublin.

From the outset of that game, right through to the All-Ireland final, Noel performed as well as he has ever done. In that game, his early battles for possession and control of the square with Tipperary danger man and captain, Eoin Kelly, laid down a clear marker of how matters would be decided between them over the course of the game. Once again, Noel's ability to redress previous discomforts was clinically and emphatically demonstrated. For a player whose entitlement to make that journey had been doubted by so many, including some of his own, this was one of his finest expeditions.

An above-average footballer Noel has represented Kilkenny at underage level. In 1997, he and Henry Shefflin played on a minor team that was only narrowly beaten by a Laois side that subsequently went on to retain the Leinster and All-Ireland titles. Were it not for his total commitment to hurling he would be a constant on the county senior team. Noel has won county Championships at all levels, including senior, with Kilmoganny, as his club is known for football purposes.

Noel's father, Andy, died young leaving his widow, Anne, with a young family of six boys and two girls and an extensive farm to manage. From an early age, the entire clan accepted that hard work was the only option, a virtue that they have all embraced and demonstrated in all aspects of their successful private and sporting lives.

Three of Noel's brothers, Jim, Tom and Canice have each experienced All-Ireland final success. Jim has won at minor (1991) and U-21 (1994) while Tom has also won at minor (1993) and junior (1995). He was defeated in the U-21 final of 1995, the junior final of 1996 and the senior final of 1998 when he was captain. Tom sustained injuries in a motor accident shortly after that game that effectively ended his career. Canice has an U-21 title (2003) and three senior titles (2007-2009). Both Jim and Tom manned the Dunamaggin full-back line with Noel in the club's senior county final win in 1997.

The omens looked positive that 2012 would be another successful one for Noel. By April, he had added Walsh Cup, Interprovincial Championship and National League titles to his collection. Sadly, however his injury jinx returned, causing him to miss the National League final win over Cork. Having lost valuable pre-Championship training during his recuperation, Noel was unable to regain his place for the commencement of the Championship. However, Noel did see action in part of Kilkenny's Leinster semi-final win over Dublin, all of their Leinster final mauling by Galway, and part of the All-Ireland semi-final demolition of Tipperary. He did not play any part in the drawn All-Ireland final.

However, Noel did see action in the replay, not once but twice. He was introduced as a blood substitute for about twelve minutes in the second half and for the final five minutes, plus added time.

For a player who has been plagued with more than his share of serious injuries, Noel has experienced a remarkably successful career, to date. Despite a curtailed involvement in 2005 and 2008, and missing out entirely in 2009, he has played over 45 inter-county Championship games, practically all at full-back. He has been a serial winner of all the game's honours, both at club and county level. He has played his beloved game in such exotic places as Rome, Buenos Aires, New York and Phoenix, Arizona, while on various Kilkenny and Leinster trips. He has been regularly honoured by the Leinster Railway Cup selectors and is a multiple All-Star award winner.

Noel lives at Tinvaun, Dunamaggin with his wife, Elaine, and family. He farms the family lands at Tinvaun and Danganmore in partnership with his brother, Jim.

Kilkenny supporters have had many memorable moments at Croke Park over the decade or so, moments that they have loudly and passionately acclaimed. The sublime skills and pure genius of Henry Shefflin, the determination and commitment of Tommy Walsh, the work rate and total focus of Derek Lyng, the versatility and class of JJ Delaney, together with the countless outstanding deeds of the other players, have all consistently brought Kilkenny followers to their feet.

However, those followers have always reserved a special space in their repository to acclaim a crucial intervention, a brave high catch, or some other feat of heroic defending by Noel, feats invariably completed with a telling clearance. Nothing plucks at the Kilkenny heartstrings more than the sight of Noel in full flight. Like Jim 'Link' Walsh, his fellow Dunamaggin clubman and All-Ireland winning full-back before him, Noel is one of Kilkenny's most popular and respected players. No explanation is required.

CAREER HIGHLIGHTS

All-Ireland senior finalist: 2000, 2002, 2003, 2004, 2006, 2007, 2008, 2009(s), 2010 and 2011

All-Ireland senior winner: 2000, 2002, 2003, 2006, 2007, 2008, 2009(s) and 2011

Leinster senior winner: 2000, 2001 2002, 2003, 2005, 2006, 2007, 2008 2009, 2010 and 2011

All-Ireland U-21 winner: 1999

Leinster U-21 winner: 1999

All-Ireland minor finalist: 1998

Leinster minor winner: 1997 and 1998

Railway Cup winner: 2002, 2003 and 2012

National League winner: 2002, 2003, 2005, 2006, 2009 and 2012

Walsh Cup winner: 2005, 2006, 2009 and 2012

County senior winner: 1997

County intermediate winner: 2000

County U-21 winner: 1996 1998 and 1999

County minor winner: 1995 and 1998

Leinster Colleges senior winner: 1998

All-Ireland Agr Colleges winner: 1999

Young Hurler of the Year: 2000

All-Star winner: 2000 2003 and 2008

County senior football winner: 2000

ALL-IRELAND WINNING TEAMS
2000
September 10
Kilkenny 5-15 Offaly 1-14
Croke Park
Attendance 61,493

Kilkenny: James McGarry (Bennettsbridge), Michael Kavanagh (St Lachtain's), Noel Hickey (Dunamaggin), Willie O'Connor (Glenmore), captain, Philly Larkin (James Stephens), Eamonn Kennedy (Dunamaggin), Peter Barry (James Stephens), Andy Comerford (O'Loughlin Gaels), Brian McEvoy (James Stephens), Denis Byrne (Graigue-Ballycallan), John Power (John Lockes), John Hoyne (Graigue-Ballycallan), Charlie Carter (Young Irelands) D J Carey (Young Irelands), Henry Shefflin (Ballyhale Shamrocks).

Subs: Martin Carey (Young Irelands), Sean Meally (Erin's Own), Aidan Cummins (Ballyhale Shamrocks), Paddy Mullally (Glenmore), Canice Brennan (Conahy Shamrocks), replaced McEvoy injured, 15 mins; John Paul Corcoran (John Lockes), Stephen Graham (The Fenians), Jimmy Coogan (Tullaroan), Eddie Brennan (Graigue-Ballycallan), replaced Brennan, 60 mins; Johnny Butler (Graigue-Ballycallan), Sean Dowling (O'Loughlin Gaels), Michael Hoyne (Graigue-Ballycallan)

2002
September 8
Kilkenny 2-20 Clare 0-19
Attendance 76,254

Kilkenny: James McGarry (Bennettsbridge), Michael Kavanagh (St Lachtain's), Noel Hickey (Dunamaggin), Philly Larkin (James Stephens), Richie Mullally (Glenmore), Peter Barry (James Stephens), JJ Delaney (The Fenians), Andy Comerford (O'Loughlin Gaels), captain, Derek Lyng (Emeralds), John Hoyne (Graigue-Ballycallan), Henry Shefflin (Ballyhale Shamrocks), Jimmy Coogan (Tullaroan), Eddie Brennan (Graigue-Ballycallan), Martin Comerford (O'Loughlin Gaels) DJ Carey (Young Irelands).

Subs: PJ Ryan (The Fenians), Sean Dowling (O'Loughlin Gaels), Charlie Carter (Young Irelands), replaced Coogan, 50 mins; Brian McEvoy (James Stephen's) replaced Hoyne, 52 mins; John Power (John Lockes) replaced Brennan, 69 mins; Pat Tennyson (Carrickshock

United), Paul Cahill (Dunamaggin), Brian Dowling (O'Loughlin Gaels), Stephen Grehan (The Fenians), Alan Geoghegan (O'Loughlin Gaels), Walter Burke (Mullinavat), James Ryall (Graigue-Ballycallan), Aidan Cummins (Ballyhale Shamrocks) Tommy Walsh (Tullaroan), Diarmuid Mackey (Mooncoin).

2003

September 14

Kilkenny 1-14 Cork 1-11

Attendance 79,383

Kilkenny: James McGarry (Bennettsbridge), Michael Kavanagh (St Lachtain's), Noel Hickey (Dunamaggin), James Ryall (Graigue-Ballycallan), Sean Dowling (O'Loughlin Gaels), Peter Barry (James Stephens), JJ Delaney (The Fenians), Derek Lyng (Emeralds) Paddy Mullally (Glenmore), Henry Shefflin (Ballyhale Shamrocks), John Hoyne (Graigue-Ballycallan), Tommy Walsh (Tullaroan), DJ Carey (Young Irelands), captain, Martin Comerford (O'Loughlin Gaels), Eddie Brennan (Graigue-Ballycallan).

Subs: PJ Ryan (The Fenians), Philly Larkin (James Stephens), Richie Mullally (Glenmore), replaced Mullally, 58 mins; Conor Phelan (Clara) replaced Walsh, injured 45 mins; Andy Comerford (O'Loughlin Gaels) replaced Ryall, 58 mins; Jimmy Coogan (Tullaroan) replaced Brennan, 64 mins; Aidan Cummins (Ballyhale Shamrocks), Jackie Tyrell (James Stephens), Ken Coogan (Tullaroan), Brian Dowling (O'Loughlin Gaels), Aidan 'Taggy' Fogarty (Emeralds), Stephen Grehan (The Fenians), Walter Burke (Mullinavat), Diarmuid Mackey (Mooncoin), Eddie Mackey (Mooncoin), John Maher (St Martin's), Willie O'Dwyer (Mullinavat), Pat Tennyson (Carrickshock United).

2006

September 3

Kilkenny 1-16 Cork 1-13

Attendance 82,275

Kilkenny: James McGarry (Bennettsbridge), Michael Kavanagh (St Lachtain's), Noel Hickey (Dunamaggin), Jackie Tyrell (James Stephens), captain, Tommy Walsh (Tullaroan), John Tennyson (Carrickshock United), James Ryall (Graigue-Ballycallan), Derek Lyng (Emeralds), James 'Cha' Fitzpatrick (Ballyhale Shamrocks), Eddie Brennan (Graigue-Ballycallan), Martin Comerford (O'Loughlin Gaels), Eoin Larkin (James

Stephens), Richie Power (Carrickshock United), Henry Shefflin (Ballyhale Shamrocks), Aidan 'Taggy' Fogarty (Emeralds).

Subs: PJ Ryan (The Fenians), Brian Hogan (O'Loughlin Gaels), Richie Mullally (Glenmore), replaced Lyng, injured, 66 mins; Michael Fennelly (Ballyhale Shamrocks), John Dalton (Carrickshock United), Stephen Maher (Tullaroan), PJ Delaney (The Fenians), Willie O'Dwyer (Mullinavat), replaced Larkin, 45 mins; Michael Rice (Carrickshock United), Eoin McCormack (James Stephens), Peter Cleere (Blacks and Whites), Austin Murphy (Clara), Sean Cummins (The Rower–Inistioge), Eoin Reid (Ballyhale Shamrocks), Seaghan O'Neill (Dunamaggin).

Unavailable through injury: JJ Delaney (The Fenians) and Donnacha Cody (James Stephens).

2007
September 2
Kilkenny 2-19 Limerick 1-15
Attendance 82,127

Kilkenny: PJ Ryan (The Fenians), Michael Kavanagh (St Lachtain's), Noel Hickey (Dunamaggin) Jackie Tyrell (James Stephens), Tommy Walsh (Tullaroan), Brian Hogan (O'Loughlin Gaels), JJ Delaney (The Fenians), Derek Lyng (Emeralds), James 'Cha' Fitzpatrick (Ballyhale Shamrocks), Willie O'Dwyer (Mullinavat), Martin Comerford (O'Loughlin Gaels), Eoin Larkin (James Stephens), Eddie Brennan (Graigue-Ballycallan), Henry Shefflin (Ballyhale Shamrocks), Aidan 'Taggy' Fogarty (Emeralds).

Subs: James McGarry (Bennettsbridge), John Tennyson (Carrickshock United), replaced Hickey, injured 25 mins; James Ryall (Graigue-Ballycallan), John Dalton (Carrickshock United), PJ Delaney (The Fenians), Sean Cummins (The Rower-Inistioge), Donnacha Cody (James Stephens), Michael Fennelly (Ballyhale Shamrocks) replaced Shefflin, injured, ht; Richie Mullally (Glenmore), replaced O'Dwyer 26 mins; Michael Rice (Carrickshock United), Eoin McCormack (James Stephens), Eoin Reid (Ballyhale Shamrocks), Peter Cleere (Blacks and Whites), Richie O'Neill (Kilmacow) Richie Hogan (Danesfort), Damien Fogarty (Erin's Own), Canice Hickey (Dunamaggin), TJ Reid (Ballyhale Shamrocks).

2008
September 7
Kilkenny 3-30 Waterford 1-13
Attendance 82,186

Kilkenny: PJ Ryan (The Fenians), Michael Kavanagh (St Lachtain's), Noel Hickey (Dunamaggin), Jackie Tyrell (James Stephens), Tommy Walsh (Tullaroan), Brian Hogan (O'Loughlin Gaels), JJ Delaney (The Fenians) James 'Cha' Fitzpatrick, (Ballyhale Shamrocks), Derek Lyng (Emeralds), Henry Shefflin (Ballyhale Shamrocks), Martin Comerford (O'Loughlin Gaels), Eoin Larkin (James Stephens), Eddie Brennan (Graigue-Ballycallan), Richie Power (Carrickshock United), Aidan 'Taggy' Fogarty (Emeralds).

Subs: James McGarry (Bennettsbridge), replaced Ryan, 61 mins; John Dalton (Carrickshock United), PJ Delaney (The Fenians), James Ryall (Graigue-Ballycallan), Canice Hickey (Dunamaggin), Donnacha Cody (James Stephens), Sean Cummins (The Rower-Inistioge), Michael Fennelly (Ballyhale Shamrocks), Richie Mullally (Glenmore), Michael Rice (Carrickshock United), Willie O'Dwyer (Mullinavat), T J Reid (Ballyhale Shamrocks), replaced Comerford, injured 44 mins; Richie Hogan (Danesfort), Eoin Reid (Ballyhale Shamrocks), David Herity (Dunamaggin), Damien Fogarty (Erin's Own) Eoin McGrath (St Martin's).

2011
September 4
Kilkenny 2-17 Tipperary 1-16, Attendance 82,214

Kilkenny: David Herity (Dunamaggin), Paul Murphy (Danesfort), Noel Hickey (Dunamaggin), Jackie Tyrell (James Stephens), Tommy Walsh (Tullaroan), Brian Hogan (O'Loughlin Gaels, (captain), JJ Delaney (The Fenians), Michael Fennelly (Ballyhale Shamrocks), Michael Rice (Carrickshock United), Eddie Brennan (Graigue-Ballycallan), Richie Power (Carrickshock United), Henry Shefflin (Ballyhale Shamrocks), Colin Fennelly (Ballyhale Shamrocks), Eoin Larkin (James Stephens), Richie Hogan (Danesfort).

Subs: PJ Ryan (The Fenians), Michael Kavanagh (St Lachtain's), John Dalton (Carrickshock United), Paddy Hogan (Danesfort), Conor Fogarty (Erin's Own), James 'Cha' Fitzpatrick (Ballyhale Shamrocks), TJ Reid (Ballyhale Shamrocks) replaced Brennan, 59 mins; John Mulhall (St Martin's) replaced Richie Hogan, 64 mins; Matthew Ruth (James Stephens) Kieran Joyce (The Rower-Inistioge), Richie Doyle (Barrow Rangers).

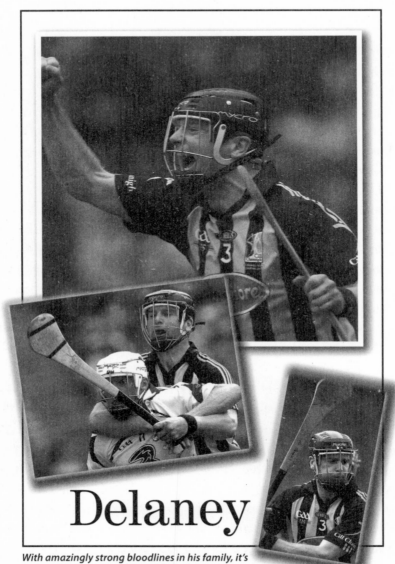

Delaney

With amazingly strong bloodlines in his family, it's no surprise that JJ Delaney has proven himself supreme in so many positions for Brian Cody's Kilkenny, including the famed No.3.

chapter 14

"In my younger days I played hurling for the pure joy of it. I don't recall having any great ambitions in the game, simply playing it was sufficient. However, as time went by, I gradually became aware of the hold that hurling had on the people of Johnstown, and, indeed, the entire county. The achievements of The Fenians in the 1960s and 1970s were constantly being talked about, as were the numerous intercounty successes of my uncles, Pat Delaney and Billie Fitzpatrick. My father, Shem, also had his days in the sun. Gradually, my interest in the game intensified.

Despite the obsession with hurling in Johnstown, the club's record at underage level was modest, to say the least. Most of my initial successes were achieved with my local school, Scoil Mhuire, being lucky enough to win four Leinster titles. Missing the All-Ireland Final in 1999 through injury was a massive disappointment. However, later in 1999, there was some consolation when I made the county minor team and won a provincial title.

In my teenage years I also became aware of the intense rivalry that existed between Kilkenny and our near neighbours, Tipperary, who always seemed to have the edge, particularly in finals. This rivalry is just as intense today and I feel very privileged to have been part of a Kilkenny team that has defeated Tipperary in two All-Ireland finals, two All-Ireland semi-finals and two National League finals. All those games were regarded as being of the highest quality, as, indeed, was the 2010 All-Ireland final when Tipperary emerged best.

I have immense regard for both the interprovincial Championship and the Fitzgibbon Cup and I feel every effort should be made to preserve and develop them. They are similar in that they both enable you to play with hurlers from different clubs and counties, and against opposition that you would not normally meet. The social aspect of each competition is very important, with friendships being formed that last a lifetime. To have captained Leinster's successful 2009 team was an immense honour. The Fitzgibbon Cup is an exciting half-way mark between underage and the more combative senior level, but is still very competitive and is always a stern test. In fact, it was following a game for Waterford Institute of Technology against Kilkenny that I was first called up for the county senior squad.

These last 12 years have been exciting for everyone involved in Kilkenny hurling. It is a tremendous honour to be selected, an honour which no player takes lightly. It is a privilege to be given the responsibility to carry on the tradition of the great players of the past and whether I do it from full-back, wing back or wherever makes no difference. To be selected to play is the target.

Sadly, it is now over 30 years since The Fenians last contested a senior county final. Now, my one, outstanding ambition is to win a county title. To retire from the game without winning a county title would be very disappointing."

JJ Delaney

—〰—

Given his birth name and his birthplace it was almost inevitable that hurling would be JJ Delaney's sporting passion. What was not inevitable was that he would develop into one of the most complete and effective wing-backs the game has seen. In the last decade alone hurling was blessed with the exploits of many other celebrated wing-backs such as Sean Og O'hAilpin, Tommy Walsh, John Gardiner, Mark Foley, Ken McGrath and Tony Browne. For JJ to be rated as at least the equal, and, in many circles, the superior, of those eminent players, is cogent evidence of his standing in the game.

Reared in the parish of Johnstown, one of the heartlands of Kilkenny hurling, JJ's bloodlines on both sides are inextricably linked with hurling success at club, county and inter-provincial levels. JJ's father, Shem, won four senior and one junior county titles with The Fenians and was a substitute on the 1974 Kilkenny All-Ireland winning team. His uncle, Pat Delaney, was one of the most feared and effective centre-forwards the game has known and was a multiple winner of all the game's premier honours, amassing four senior All-Irelands, two All-Star awards, five senior county titles and five Railway Cup titles in a glittering career. JJ's mother, Joan, who sadly died in July 1990, was a sister of Billy Fitzpatrick, one of the most outstanding exponents of the traditional Kilkenny style of forward play and a multiple All-Ireland medallist at senior, U-21, minor and colleges, also experiencing successes at Railway Cup, National League and county Championship levels. And, finally, JJ's cousin, PJ Delaney, also won All-Ireland medals in all grades before his career was callously and cruelly cut short following an assault in Thurles in September, 1999.

JJ was born on March 6, 1982. It is surprising, considering the devotion towards hurling in the area, that his club underage years went largely unrewarded, his only success being the 1995 North U-16 championship win. At schools level, JJ experienced better results, winning two junior and two senior Leinster Vocational titles with Colaiste Mhuire, Johnstown.

The first major club title that came JJ's direction was the 1997 Roinn B, U-21 championship. In 1999, he won a Leinster minor title but an All-Ireland semi-final defeat by Galway stymied loftier ambitions. Impressive performances at various levels with The Fenians and with WIT throughout 2000 propelled JJ into the gaze of the hurling public, and, by extension, the county management

When Kilkenny began the defence of their championship titles against Offaly in June 2001, JJ was the only one of the starting 15 who had not previously seen any championship action at senior level. He then played at left corner-back, a position he occupied throughout the championship, which ended in a shattering defeat by Galway in the All-Ireland semi-final. While the nature of that defeat was clearly a setback to the development of the team, on a personal level the year was relatively successful for JJ − a first senior provincial title win, and a place on the team practically assured. He had yet to reach his 20th birthday.

For the major 2002 competitions, JJ was moved to left-half-back, a position that best suited his more adventurous, attacking style. The switch benefited both team and player with the National League and Championship double achieved in emphatic fashion. JJ's game had developed to such a level of excellence and maturity that was almost improbable, but his best years were ahead of him.

The hurling year of 2003 was memorable for Kilkenny, and even more so for JJ. He began the year by winning his first Fitzgibbon Cup medal with a Waterford Institute of Technology side that included future inter-county players such as Paul Curran, Brian Dowling, Setanta O'hAilpin, Ollie Moran, Conor Phelan, Mick Jacob and Ken Coogan. Waterford's opponents in that final were a Cork Institute of Technology side that included Kilkenny's Jackie Tyrell and Aidan Fogarty, Cork players Ronan Curran, John Gardiner, Martin Coleman, Brian Murphy and Kieran Murphy.

Kilkenny's All-Ireland and League titles were retained, with JJ being selected as Texaco Hurler of the Year. and All-Star Hurler of the Year. Though he began the championship at left corner-back against Dublin (best remembered as the game that catapulted Charlie Carter into his self-imposed, highly publicised retirement), JJ was later restored to left half-back where he excelled for the remainder of that successful year. In a team comprising an array of brilliant hurlers, most of whom had several successful years service behind them, it spoke volumes for JJ's standing in the game, and the excellence of his year-long performances that he won those individual awards in what was only his third year on the team

An incident in the second half of the All-Ireland final perfectly illustrates the vital part JJ played in Kilkenny's win. Cork corner-forward Setanta O'hAilpin had scored a possible game-winning goal midway through the second half and thereafter looked as if he could almost single-handedly win the match. The Kilkenny management responded to the O'hAilpin threat by moving JJ back to left corner-back to police him. It is arguable that JJ's curbing of O'hAilpin was as significant a contributory factor in Kilkenny's ultimate win as Martin Comerford's and Henry Shefflin's late scores. Within days of that win JJ starred in Kilkenny's U-21 All-Ireland final win over Galway.

Apart from winning a second Fitzgibbon Cup medal, 2004 was not a memorable year for JJ. Kilkenny's two national titles and their provincial title were lost, with the eight-points defeat by Cork in the All-Ireland final being a particularly chastening experience. In the Leinster semi-final defeat by Wexford, JJ lined out at left corner-back, while, for the remaining six championship games, he manned the left half-back position.

By the summer of 2005 the omens for Kilkenny looked positive. The National League and Leinster titles were retained in a manner that suggested that perhaps the lethargy and the drop in standard of the previous year were but bad memories. However, for the second time in that half decade, Kilkenny came unstuck against Galway in the All-Ireland semi-final, losing by a goal in a 5-18 to 4-18 scoring spectacular.

Due to Noel Hickey's new injury problems in the early stages of 2006, JJ played at full-back in Kilkenny's retention of the National League and the Leinster semi-final win. Despite Hickey's return, JJ held the full-back position for the provincial final and All-Ireland quarter-final wins, with Hickey positioned at left corner-back. For the All-Ireland semi-final win against Clare, the players swapped positions. Before the All-Ireland final, as speculation arose as to which of them would be full-back against Cork, fate took over with JJ suffering a serious knee injury in training, one that took him out of contention, not only for a final place but also out of the game for the remainder of the year. Curiously, in the euphoria that surrounded Kilkenny's subsequent unforgettable win, JJ's loss to the team was practically overlooked. Never was Brian Cody's insistence on maintaining a competitive squad system more clinically justified.

Kilkenny's only blemish in 2007 was a defeat by Waterford in the National League final. With Noel Hickey finally free of injury and firmly ensconced at full-back, JJ was restored to his favourite No.7 position where he excelled in Kilkenny's successful defence of their championship titles, giving a typically faultless display in the All-Ireland final against Limerick.

As Kilkenny set out in 2008 in pursuit of a three-in-a-row they did so with JJ once more deputising for the again recuperating Noel Hickey. The Dunamaggin man did not return to action until the All-Ireland semi-final allowing JJ to again revert to his left half-back position. Having overcome Cork with a very ruthless but disciplined display, Kilkenny then went on to demolish Waterford in the final, with JJ imperious at left half-back

JJ began the 2009 hurling season again deputising for the recuperating

Noel Hickey in the full-back position. However, this year was different from other years in that, despite valiant efforts by Hickey to regain his place, the management team retained JJ at full-back throughout the year, one in which another League-Championship double was achieved, the fourth time under Brian Cody's leadership. JJ's All-Ireland final duel with Tipperary's leading forward, Eoin Kelly, was one of the features of a memorable game, one that concluded with a late Kilkenny scoring blitz to take the honours, the first authentic four-in-a-row of All-Ireland senior title wins. JJ's part in his team's historic achievement cannot be overstated. Rarely has a player displayed such adept versatility on the biggest stage. Not since John O'Keeffe and Sean Walsh of Kerry's 1970s-1980s 'Golden Era' has an natural outfield player demonstrated an ability to so comfortably and effectively perform in the more restricted confines of the full-back position in the white heat of an All-Ireland final.

Kilkenny's valiant efforts to achieve a fifth successive All-Ireland title came badly unstuck in the in the final against Tipperary. With Noel Hickey restored to full back, JJ was once again operating at left half-back. In the weeks leading up to the final, fate intervened to reduce Kilkenny's chances of victory, as a succession of injuries bedevilled the team. Tommy Walsh, John Tennyson, Henry Shefflin and Brian Hogan, players crucial to Kilkenny, all suffered injuries that, in the case of Walsh and Tennyson, made them less effective than usual, while Shefflin lasted a mere 12 minutes, with Hogan missing out entirely. Yet, despite that carnage, Kilkenny were still competitive well into the closing minutes, the game only slipping from their grasp, courtesy of a late Tipperary scoring blitz.

Despite their injury-crippled side's brave effort to achieve the historic five successive titles, deep down many Kilkenny followers feared that the good days were over. After all, the pendulum had appeared to have swung decidedly in Tipperary's way. They were a younger team, and had played with the same ferocity and intensity that Kilkenny had brought to a fine art over the previous five years. Tipperary, it seemed could only improve; Kilkenny, it was feared, could hardly get much better than they had been, and critically, it was unclear if their playmaker, spiritual leader and chief scorer, Henry Shefflin, would even make it back, not to say be the player he had been. The omens were not positive – 2011 could be a difficult year.

Almost by accident Kilkenny reached The National League final where they took a severe drubbing from Dublin. No more than the rest of the team JJ, playing at full-back didn't distinguish himself in that game. For the provincial semi-final against Wexford he again manned the square, and looked far more comfortable than his corner men, Noel Hickey and Jackie Tyrell.

It appeared that the management, despite an epidemic of chopping and changing of their resources since the beginning of the year, still did not appear to have decided on a settled full-back line. However, for the last two games of the championship, starting with the All-Ireland semi-final, Noel Hickey was restored to full-back, flanked by relative newcomer, Paul Murphy and a re-energised Jackie Tyrell, with JJ reverting to his favourite left half-back position. The rest, as the saying goes, is history. The new full-back line held a succession of full-forward lines in non-scoring vice-like grips en route to Kilkennys 33rd, and one of their most satisfying, title wins. JJ did as he has always done, and gave an exhibition of wing-back play. In a back line that excelled in all facets of defending, JJ was irrepressible. His ability to out-field much taller opponents defied logic, while his covering, his sweeping up, his blocking, his accurate deliveries out of defence, were inspiring. He more than held his own in those early physical exchanges where players like to lay down markers as to how the afternoon will be played out. He was a worthy winner of RTE's Man of the Match Award.

There was little indication during the early months of the 2012 season that JJ would finish the year at full-back. With Noel Hickey performing well at full-back, Kilkenny won the Walsh Cup and a Kilkenny-dominated defence helped Leinster to the Interprovincial Championship. However, a recurrence of Noel's injury problems saw JJ restored to full-back for the National League final win. He has remained at full-back since then, missing only the Leinster final, through injury.

In the replay of the All-Ireland final, Kilkenny refused to be influenced by Galway's tactics as they had been in the drawn game. The employment of a more conventional defensive line-up suited all the Kilkenny defenders, not least JJ, who gave a faultless display of last-line defending.

JJ's strengths are so varied and many that it is difficult to pigeonhole what his main strengths are. While his grip is something that could horrify some purists, all other facets of his game are pure poetry in motion. Though not the tallest of men his ability to consistently dominate the aerial exchanges is simply astounding. Like all great players, he never seems under pressure and appears to have acres of space and plenty of time to get in his stroke. He also has a fluid movement of foot. Consequently he rarely, if ever caught in possession, gets hooked, blocked down or miss-hits the ball. His ground strokes are as measured and accurate as to satisfy the demands of a low-handicap golfer. His ability to perform to the highest standard in different positions in the cauldron of an All-Ireland final is proven, and unique in modern times. Occasionally, in the past, players have suffered through their versatility, principally because they never quite mastered any one position. Not so JJ, who seems totally unencumbered by the number on his jersey. He has won All-Star awards in three positions, three at left half-back and one each at full-back and right half-back. In addition JJ has won Railway Cup medals with Leinster from both the centre-half and left half-back positions

From Kilkenny's emergence as a hurling county in the early years of the 1900s they have been blessed with the ability to consistently produce outstanding goalkeepers, irrepressible full-backs, heroic centre-backs, long-striking and long-striding mid-fielders and an assortment of illustrious forwards. To that menu, surely, must be added the position of left half-back, which has, over the years, been occupied by such icons as Eddie Doyle, Dick Grace, Paddy Phelan, Johnny McGovern, Martin Coogan, Willie O'Connor, and, more recently, by JJ. An impressive cast by any standard.

Put simply, JJ, a construction economics graduate from WIT, is an all-round outstanding hurler, and is as good a defender as Kilkenny has ever produced. That's more than sufficient.

CAREER HIGHLIGHTS

All-Ireland senior finalist: 2002, 2003, 2004 2007, 2008, 2009, 2010, 2011 and 2012
All-Ireland senior winner: 2002, 2003, 2006(s), 2007, 2008, 2009, 2011 and 2012
Leinster senior winner: 2001, 2002, 2003, 2005, 2006, 2007, 2008, 2009, 2010 and 2011

All-Ireland U-21 winner: 2003

Leinster U-21 winner: 2003

National League winner: 2002, 2003, 2005, 2006, 2009 and 2012

Railway Cup winner: 2002, 2009 (captain) and 2012

Leinster minor winner: 1999

Fitzgibbon Cup winner 2003 and 2004

Walsh Cup winner: 2006, 2007, 2008, 2009 and 2012

County U-21 winner: 1999

Texaco Hurler of the Year winner: 2003

All-Star Hurler of the Year: 2003

All-Star Award winner: 2003, 2004, 2006, 2007 and 2010

Leinster Vocational championship winner (junior and senior): 1996-1999

ALL-IRELAND WINNING TEAMS

2009
September 6
Kilkenny 2-22 Tipperary 0-23
Croke Park
Attendance 82,106

Kilkenny: PJ Ryan (The Fenians), Michael Kavanagh (St Lachtains), JJ Delaney (The Fenians), Jackie Tyrell (James Stephens), Tommy Walsh (Tullaroan), Brian Hogan (O'Loughlin Gaels), John Tennyson (Carrickshock United), Derek Lyng (Emeralds), Michael Rice (Carrickshock United), Eddie Brennan (Graigue-Ballycallan), Eoin Larkin (James Stephens), Richie Power (Carrickshock United), Richie Hogan (Danesfort), Henry Shefflin (Ballyhale Shamrocks), Aidan Fogarty (Emeralds).

Subs: David Herity (Dunamaggin), Noel Hickey (Dunamaggin), James Ryall (Graigue-Ballycallan), James 'Cha' Fitzpatrick (Ballyhale Shamrocks), Michael Fennelly (Ballyhale Shamrocks), captain, replaced Lyng, 52 mins; Martin Comerford (O'Loughlin Gaels), replaced Hogan, 55 mins; TJ Reid (Ballyhale Shamrocks), replaced Fogarty 50 mins; Sean Cummins (The Rower-Inistioge), Canice Hickey (Dunamaggin), PJ Delaney (The Fenians) Damien Fogarty (Erin's Own), Willie O'Dwyer (Mullinavat) Eoin Reid (Ballyhale Shamrocks), Michael Grace (The Rower-Inistioge).

2012

September 30
Kilkenny 3-22 Galway 3-11
Attendance, 82,646.

Kilkenny: David Herity (Dunamaggin), Paul Murphy (Danesfort), JJ Delaney (The Fenians), Jackie Tyrrell (James Stephens), Tommy Walsh (Tullaroan), Brian Hogan (O'Loughlin Gaels), Kieran Joyce, (The Rower-Inistioge), Michael Fennelly, (Ballyhale Shamrocks), Richie Hogan (Danesfort), Cillian Buckley, (Dicksboro), Richie Power, (Carrickshock), Eoin Larkin (James Stephens), captain, TJ Reid, (Ballyhale Shamrocks), Walter Walsh, (Tullogher-Rosbercon), Henry Sheflin, (Ballyhale Shamrocks).

Subs: Eoin Murphy, (Glenmore), Noel Hickey (Dunamaggin), blood substitute for Delaney, 49 min. replacement for Joyce, 65 min. Richir Doyle (Barrow Rangers), Conor Fogarty, (Erin's Own), John Tennyson, (Carrickshock), Paddy Hogan (Danesfort), Aidan Fogarty, (Emeralds), Replaced Reid, injured 65 min. Colin Fennelly, (Ballyhale Shamrocks), replaced Walter Walsh, 59 min. Matthew Ruth, (James Stephens), Mark Kelly, (O'Loughlin Gaels), Joe Brennan, (St Patrick's), Michael Rice, (Carrickshock), Lester Ryan (Clara), Thomas Breen, (St Martin's), Mark Bergin, (O'Loughlin Gaels), Willie Phelan (Dunnamaggin).

Epilogue

FULL-BACKS IN ALL-IRELAND FINAL DEFEATS

1916

Tom Hanrahan (Dicksboro)

Originally from Kiljames, Thomastown. Tom's first hurling success was in 1913 when winning the county junior Championship with Mong, a local team. He subsequently joined Dicksboro with whom he played in the losing 1915 county senior final. When Jack Rochford withdrew from the team prior to the 1916 All-Ireland final, Tom was his direct replacement.

Tom's last Championship outing was in Kilkenny's 1917 Leinster final defeat by Dublin.

1926, 1931 and 1936

Peter O'Reilly (Dicksboro)

1937

Podge Byrne (Dicksboro)

Podge Byrne, who won county titles in 1923 and 1926, made his Championship debut in 1927 against Laois at St James' Park in July 1927. He and his brother, Eddie, were members of the successful Kilkenny team of the 1930s, winning All-Ireland titles in 1932,1933 and 1935, and the 1932/33 National League.

As one of Kilkenny's leading defenders, Podge was a regular on Leinster Railway Cup teams, winning inter-provincial titles in 1932, 1933 and in 1936, when he deputised at full-back for his injured clubmate, Peter O'Reilly.

Following the retirement of Peter O'Reilly in 1936, the Kilkenny selectors switched Podge, a natural half-back, to full-back where he played throughout the 1937 Championship. He retired from inter-county hurling following Kilkenny's defeat in that year's All-Ireland final.

1940

Paddy Larkin (Eire Og)

1945

Mick Kelly (Mooncoin)

From Ballinaroughry, Kilmacow, Mick played senior Championship hurling initially with Mooncoin, and later with Dicksboro. He was Kilkenny's first choice full-back for only the 1945 season, winning a provincial title and playing in the losing All-Ireland final.

For the 1946 Championship, Mick was relegated to the substitutes bench, his place being taken by Hugginstown's Mick Butler, who had returned to the county colours following a very successful career with Dublin.

Mick's last Championship outing with Kilkenny was when he replaced the injured Butler in the second half of that year's All-Ireland final.

1946

Mick Butler (Faughs, Dublin)

Originally from Lismatigue, Hugginstown, Mick experienced a very successful career with Dublin with whom he won the 1938 All-Ireland title, and four provincial titles, 1938, 1941, 1942 and 1944. He was full-back on Leinster's winning 1941 Railway Cup team and won six senior county titles with Faughs.

Mick transferred back to Kilkenny for the 1946 Championship, which ended in a defeat by Cork in the All-Ireland final. That game was his last for Kilkenny.

Though he was included in Kilkenny's lineout to face Cork in February, 1947, in the National League, he did not play that game as he did not again declare to play for his native county.

1950

Pat 'Diamond' Hayden (Eire Og)

1959

Jim 'Link' Walsh (Dunamaggin)

1964

Pa Dillon (St Lachtains)

1966

Jimmy Lynch (Mooncoin)

Full-back and captain in 1966, Jimmy won All-Ireland senior medals in 1967 (full-forward) and 1969 (sub). He also won an All-Ireland minor title in 1960.

Jimmy experienced a successful club career, winning county titles at minor (1960), junior (1961) and senior (1965).

Honoured by the Leinster selectors in 1966, Jimmy captained Kilkenny to National League and Oireachtas Tournament successes later that year.

1971

Pa Dillon (St Lachtains)

1973
Nickey Orr (The Fenians)

1978
Fan Larkin (James Stephens)

Son of the legendary Paddy Larkin, Fan not only replicated his father's achievements, but actually surpassed them. Having won his first All-Ireland medal in 1963, Fan paid a heavy price for Kilkenny's All-Ireland final capitulation against Tipperary the following year, not again appearing on a Kilkenny Championship panel until June, 1970. However, that emerging decade was to prove a bountiful one for Fan as at club, county and provincial he experienced tremendous success. (See below)

An accomplished footballer, Fan represented Kilkenny at all grades. He won three senior county titles, two with Clann na Gael and one with The Village. (James Stephens' sister club).

Like his father, Fan made light of his small stature, giving some of his more memorable displays against such towering figures as Ray Cummins, Joe McKenna Tony Doran and John Connolly.

Though a committed James Stephens man, Fan also played senior Championship hurling with Eire Og, a city-based club with a proud tradition, but which, sadly, disbanded in the late 1960s.

All-Ireland S H C (5) 1963, 1972, 1974, 1975 and 1979

Leinster SHC (9) 1963, 1964, 1971, 1972, 1973, 1974 1975 1978 and 1979

Railway Cup (6) 1972, 1973, 1974, 1975, 1977 and 1979 (captain)

All-Star Awards (4) 1973, 1974, 1976 and 1978

All-Ireland Club (2) 1975/76 and 1981/82

Leinster Club (2) 1975/76 and 1981/ 82

Kilkenny SHC (4) 1969, 1975, 1976 and 1981

Leinster MHC 1959

Kilkenny MHC 1957

Kilkenny SFC (3) 1963 and 1964 (Clann Na Gael) 1976 (The Village)

Kilkenny JFC 1962 (Clann Na Gael).

1987
Paddy Prendergast (Clara)

1991
John Henderson (The Fenians)

The third member of the Henderson family to represent Kilkenny at senior Championship level, John won three senior All-Ireland titles, 1979 (left corner-back), 1982 and 1983 (both at right corner-back). Apart from bearing the pure Henderson blood he also carried his own impressive array of talents that proved that he did not need to depend solely on lineage to make his way at the top level.

John won minor and U-21 All-Ireland

titles in 1975 and 1977, respectively. In a senior career that lasted from 1979 to 1991 John also won four National League and six Leinster titles.

In 1988 he became the third member of the family to win a Railway Cup medal. He won his sole county senior title in 1977, also playing in the losing finals of 1978, 1981 and 1993.

1998
Pat O'Neill (Young Irelands)

Pat arrived at senior Championship level following a very impressive underage career, with All-Ireland senior colleges (1988) All-Ireland minor (1988) and All-Ireland U-21 (1990) titles already to his credit. Curiously, while it was at centre-back, where he won his two senior All-Ireland medals, 1992 and 1993, it was as a wing forward that he began his senior inter-county Championship career against Wexford in the 1991 Leinster semi-final.

With county colleagues, DJ Carey and Charlie Carter, Pat was one of the driving forces behind his club's rise from intermediate status to become senior

county champions of 1996. Given such riches of talent it was surprising that the club only added one more senior title to their inventory.

Pat also played at centre back in Kilkenny's defeat by Cork in the 1999 All-Ireland final.

He won both a Railway Cup medal and an All-Star award in 1993.

1999
Canice Brennan (Conahy Shamrocks)

With defeats in the All-Ireland finals of 1998 and 1999, Canice must have despaired of ever garnering a winner's medal. However, Kilkenny's comprehensive · win in the 2000 final, part of which he played as a substitute, filled that vacuum.

Canice won senior Colleges All-Ireland titles in 1989 and 1990, and a minor All-Ireland, also in 1990. He came on as a replacement in Kilkenny's National League final win over Clare in 1995.

2004 and 2010
Noel Hickey (Dunamaggin)

KILKENNY'S CHAMPIONSHIP RECORD 1887 TO 2012

1887 No Leinster Championship. County champions, Tullaroan, were defeated in third round of open draw All-Ireland Championship by Thurles.

1888 County champions, Mooncoin won Leinster Championship defeating Dublin's Kickhams. The All-Ireland Championship was not completed due to US tour by elite hurlers, 'The American Invasion.'

1889 County champions, Tullaroan, conceded a walkover to Dublin's Kickhams in the Leinster Championship.

1890 County champions, Bennettsbridge, lost to Castlebridge, Wexford, in Leinster Championship.

1891 No Kilkenny Championship. Kilkenny did not compete in Leinster Championship.

1892 No Kilkenny Championship. Kilkenny did not compete in Leinster Championship.

1893 County champions, Confederation, were sole team to enter Leinster Championship and received bye into All-Ireland final but were defeated by Cork's Blackrock. This was the first year of open representation on the county team.

1894 County champions, Confederation, conceded walkover to Dublin's Rapparees.

1895 Kilkenny (Tullaroan-Threecastles) won Leinster Championship. Defeated in All-Ireland final by Tipperary's Tubberadora.

1896 County champions, Confederation, represented Kilkenny - defeated in Leinster final by Dublin's Commercials following a replay.

1897 County champions. Tullaroan. Won Leinster Championship – defeated by Limerick's Killfane in All-Ireland final.

1898 County champions. Threecastles. won Leinster Championship: defeated in All-Ireland final by Tipperary's Tubberadora.

1899 County champions, Tullaroan, conceded walkover to Dublin's Commercials in Leinster final.

1900 County champions, Mooncoin, won Leinster Championship: defeated in All-Ireland semi-final by Tipperary's Two Mile Borris.

1901 County champions, Tullaroan, defeated by Wexford's Blackwater in Leinster semi-final.

1902 County champions, Tullaroan, defeated in Leinster final by Dublin's Faughs.

Hereafter no reference to clubs, county only

1903 Leinster champions: defeated by Cork in All-Ireland 'Home' final.

1904 Leinster and All-Ireland champions: defeated Dublin and Cork in respective finals.

1905 Leinster and All-Ireland champions: defeated Dublin and Cork in respective finals.

1906 Leinster finalists: defeated by Dublin.

1907 Leinster and All-Ireland champions: defeated Dublin and Cork in respective finals.

1908 Conceded walkover to Dublin in Leinster final. Railway Shield issue.

1909 Leinster and All-Ireland champions – Defeated Laois and Tipperary in respective finals.

1910 Leinster semi-finalists – defeated by Dublin.

1911 Leinster and All-Ireland champions – defeated Dublin in Leinster final and awarded All-Ireland title when Limerick refused to play rescheduled final.

1912 Leinster and All-Ireland champions – defeated Dublin and Cork in respective finals.

1913 Leinster All-Ireland champions – defeated Dublin (replay) and Tipperary in respective finals.

1914 Leinster finalists – defeated by Laois.

1915 Leinster semi-finalists – defeated by Laois.

1916 Leinster champions and All-Ireland finalists – defeated Wexford but lost to Tipperary in respective finals.

1917 Leinster finalists – defeated by Dublin.

1918 First-round defeat by Dublin

1919 Leinster finalists – defeated by Dublin.

1920 Leinster finalists – defeated by Dublin.

1921 Leinster finalists – defeated by Dublin.

1922 Leinster and All-Ireland champions – defeated Dublin and Tipperary in respective finals.

1923 Leinster champions and All-Ireland semi-finalists – defeated Dublin but lost to Galway, respectively.

1924 Leinster semi-finalists – defeated by Dublin.

1925 Leinster champions and All-Ireland semi-finalists – awarded Leinster title following objection to Dublin, but subsequently defeated by Galway.

1926 Leinster champions and All-Ireland finalists – defeated Offaly but lost to Cork respectively.

1927 Leinster finalists – defeated by Dublin

1928 First round – defeated by Dublin.

1929 Expelled from Leinster Championship after defeating Dublin in Leinster final. Dublin also expelled. Kilkenny subsequently were nominated to represent Leinster in the All-Ireland series, but were defeated by Galway in the semi-final.

1930 Leinster semi-finalists – defeated by Laois.

1931 Leinster champions and All-Ireland finalists – defeated Laois but lost to Cork (after three games) in respective finals.

1932 Leinster and All-Ireland champions – defeated Dublin and Clare in respective finals.

1933 Leinster and All-Ireland champions – defeated Dublin and Limerick in respective finals.

1934 Leinster finalists – defeated by Dublin.

1935 Leinster and All-Ireland champions – defeated Laois and Limerick in respective finals.

1936 Leinster champions and All-Ireland finalists – defeating Laois but lost to Limerick in respective finals.

1937 Leinster champions and All-Ireland finalists – defeated Westmeath but lost to Tipperary in respective finals.

1938 Leinster finalists – defeated by Dublin.

1939 Leinster and All-Ireland champions – defeated Dublin and Cork in respective finals.

1940 Leinster champions and All-Ireland finalists – defeated Dublin but lost to Limerick in respective finals.

1941 Leinster finalists – defeated by Dublin.

1942 Leinster finalists – defeated by Dublin.

1943 Leinster champions and All-Ireland semi-finalists – defeated Dublin but lost to Antrim respectively.

1944 Defeated by Wexford in Leinster semi-final.

1945 Leinster champions and All-Ireland finalists – defeated Dublin but lost to Tipperary in respective finals.

1946 Leinster champions and All-Ireland finalists – defeated Dublin but lost to Cork in respective finals.

1947 Leinster and All-Ireland champions – defeated Dublin and Cork in respective finals.

1948 Leinster semi-finalists – defeated by Laois.

1949 Leinster finalists – defeated by Laois.

1950 Leinster champions and All-Ireland finalists – defeated Wexford but lost to Tipperary in respective finals.

1951 Leinster semi-finalists – defeated by Laois.

1952 Leinster semi-finalists – defeated by Wexford.

1953 Leinster champions and All-Ireland semi-finalists – defeated Wexford but lost to Galway in respective games.

1954 Leinster semi-finalists – defeated by Wexford.

1955 Leinster finalists – defeated by Wexford.

1956 Leinster finalists – defeated by Wexford.

1957 Leinster and All-Ireland champions – defeated Wexford and Waterford in respective finals.

1958 Leinster champions and All-Ireland semi-finalists – defeated Wexford but lost to Tipperary in respective games.

1959 Leinster champions and All-Ireland finalists – defeated Dublin but lost to Waterford (replay) in respective finals.

1960 Leinster finalists – defeated by Wexford.

1961 Leinster semi-finalists – defeated by Wexford.

1962 Leinster finalists – defeated by Wexford.

1963 Leinster and All-Ireland champions – defeated Dublin and Waterford in respective finals.

1964 Leinster champions and All-Ireland finalists – defeated Dublin but lost to Tipperary in respective finals.

1965 Leinster finalists – defeated by Wexford.

1966 Leinster champions and All-Ireland finalists, defeated Wexford but lost to Cork in respective games.

1967 Leinster and All-Ireland champions – defeated Wexford and Tipperary in respective finals.

1968 Leinster finalists – defeated by Wexford.

1969 Leinster and All-Ireland champions – defeated Offaly and Cork in respective finals.

1970 Leinster finalists – defeated by Wexford.

1971 Leinster champions and All-Ireland finalists – defeated Wexford but lost to Tipperary in respective finals.

1972 Leinster and All-Ireland champions – defeated Wexford (replay) and Cork in respective finals.

1973 Leinster champions and All-Ireland finalists – defeated Wexford but lost to Limerick in respective finals.

1974 Leinster and All-Ireland champions – defeated Wexford and Limerick in respective finals.

1975 Leinster and All-Ireland champions – defeated Wexford and Galway in respective finals.

1976 Leinster finalists – defeated by Wexford.

1977 Leinster finalists – defeated by Wexford.

1978 Leinster champions and All-Ireland finalists – defeated Wexford but lost to Cork in respective finals.

1979 Leinster and All-Ireland champions – defeated Wexford and Galway respective finals.

1980 Leinster finalists – defeated by Offaly.

1981 Leinster semi-finalists – defeated by Wexford.

1982 Leinster and All-Ireland champions – defeated Offaly and Cork in respective finals.

1983 Leinster and All-Ireland champions – defeated Offaly and Cork in respective finals.

1984 Leinster semi-finalists – defeated by Wexford.

1985 Leinster semi-finalists – defeated by Offaly.

1986 Leinster champions and All-Ireland semi-finalists – defeated Offaly but lost to Galway in respective games.

1987 Leinster champions and All-Ireland finalists – defeated Offaly but lost to Galway in respective finals.

1988 Leinster semi-finalists – defeated by Wexford.

1989 Leinster finalists – defeated by Offaly.

1990 Leinster semi-finalists – defeated by Offaly.

1991 Leinster champions and All-Ireland finalists – defeated Dublin but lost to Tipperary in respective finals.

1992 Leinster and All-Ireland champions – defeated Wexford and Cork in respective finals.

1993 Leinster and All-Ireland champions – defeated Wexford (replay) and Galway in respective finals.

1994 Leinster semi-finalists – defeated by Offaly.

1995 Leinster finalists – defeated by Offaly.

1996 Leinster semi-finalists – defeated by Wexford.

Introduction of the Qualifier System

1997 Leinster finalists and All-Ireland semi-finalists – defeated by Wexford and Clare respectively.

1998 Leinster champions and All-Ireland finalists – defeated Offaly in Leinster final, but lost to them in All-Ireland final.

1999 Leinster champions and All-Ireland finalists – defeated Offaly but lost to Cork in respective finals.

2000 Leinster and All-Ireland champions – defeated Offaly in both finals.

2001 Leinster champions and All-Ireland finalists – defeated Wexford but lost to Galway in respective games.

2002 Leinster and All-Ireland champions – defeated Wexford and Clare in respective finals.

2003 Leinster and All-Ireland champions – defeated Wexford and Cork in respective finals.

2004 Leinster semi-finalists and All-Ireland finalists – defeated by Wexford and Cork in respective games.

2005 Leinster champions and All-Ireland semi-finalists – defeated Wexford but lost to Galway in respective games.

2006 Leinster and All-Ireland champions – defeated Wexford and Cork in respective finals.

2007 Leinster and All-Ireland champions – defeated Wexford and Limerick in respective finals.

2008 Leinster and All-Ireland champions – defeated Wexford and Waterford in respective finals.

2009 Leinster and All-Ireland champions – defeated Dublin and Tipperary in respective finals.

2010 Leinster champions and All-Ireland finalists – defeated Galway but lost to Tipperary in respective finals.

2011 Leinster and All-Ireland champions – defeated Dublin and Tipperary in respective finals.

2012 Leinster finalists and All-Ireland Champions – defeated by Galway and defeated Galway in respective finals.

KILKENNY CHAMPIONSHIP FULL-BACKS, 1904 - 2012

1904 – 1916

Jack Rochford – Threecastles, also played with Erin's Own (city) and Tullaroan.
Tom Hanrahan – Dicksboro, played in All-Ireland Final 1916.

1917

Tom Hanrahan – Dicksboro.

1918 – 1925

John Holohan – Played with Crosspatrick, Johnstown and Tullaroan.

1926

Peter O'Reilly – Dicksboro. Played in Leinster final, All-Ireland semi-final and All-Ireland final.
Wattie Dunphy – Mooncoin. Played in Leinster semi-final.

1927 – 1928

Peter O'Reilly – Dicksboro.

1929

Padge Byrne – Dicksboro.

1930

Martin Murphy – Mooncoin.

1931 – 1936

Peter O'Reilly – Dicksboro.

1937

Padge Byrne – Dicksboro.

1938

Billy Burke – Tullaroan. Also played with Eire Og and James Stephens.

1939 – 1941

Paddy Larkin – Eire Og. Also played with Tullaroan and James Stephens.
Bob Aylward – Carrickshock played in 1939 Leinster semi-final.

1942

Bob Aylward – Carrickshock.

1943

Paddy Larkin – James Stephens. Also played with Eire Og and Tullaroan.

1944

Paddy Grace – Dicksboro. Also played with Carrickshock and James Stephens.

1945

Mick Kelly – Mooncoin. Also played with Dicksboro. Originally from Ballinaroughry, Kilmacow.
Peter Blanchfield – James Stephens. Also played with Tullaroan and Eire Og. Played in first round win over Wexford.

1946

Mick Butler – Faughs, Dublin, and formerly of Hugginstown.

Mick Kelly – Dicksboro. Also played with Mooncoin; played in the All-Ireland semi-final against Antrim and came on as substitute in second half of All-Ireland final against Cork.

1947-1954

Pat 'Diamond' Hayden - Eire Og. Also played with Castle Rovers and Northern Selection.

Ned Kavanagh – Tullaroan. Originally from Urlingford. Came on as substitute in second half of 1947 All-Ireland final.

Jack Galway – Bennettsbridge. Came on as substitute in second half of 1954 Leinster semi-final.

1955 – 1956

John Maher – Crokes, Dublin. Formally of Freshford. Also played with, Roger Casement's, Birmingham.

1957 – 1959

Jim 'Link' Walsh – Dunamaggin.

1960

Pa Dillon – St Lachtains, Freshford.

1961

Jim Hennessy – Tullaroan.

John Maher – Crokes, Dublin. Formerly of Freshford. Also played with Roger Casement's, Birmingham. Played in second half of Leinster semi-final.

1962

Jim 'Link' Walsh – Dunamaggin.

1963

Cha Whelan – Thomastown.

Jim 'Link' Walsh – Dunamaggin. Played in first half of Leinster semi-final.

1964 – 1965

Pa Dillon – St Lachtain's, Freshford.

Jim Lynch – Mooncoin. Played in 1964 Leinster semi-final.

1966

Jim Lynch – Mooncoin.

1967 – 1972

Pa Dillon – St Lachtain's, Freshford

Ted Carroll – Lisdowney Played in 1971 Leinster semi-final.

Johnny Walsh – Mooncoin. Played in 1972 Leinster semi-final.

1973 – 1976

Nicky Orr – Fenians.

1977

Pat Henderson – Fenians.

1978
Philip 'Fan' Larkin – James Stephens.

1979
Phil 'Fan' Larkin – James Stephens. Played in Leinster Championship.
Paddy Prendergast – Clara. Played in part of Leinster final and all of All-Ireland final.

1980
Brian Cody – James Stephens.

1981
Jim Moran – Muckalee-Ballyfoyle Rangers.
Brian Cody – James Stephens. Came on as substitute in Leinster semi-final.

1982 – 1983
Brian Cody – James Stephens.

1984
Dick O'Hara – Thomastown United.

1985
Paudhi Brennan – Conahy Shamrocks.

1986
John Henderson – Fenians.

1987
Paddy Prendergast – Clara.

1988
Ger Henderson – Fenians.

1989
Pat Dwyer – Carrickshock United.

1990 – 1991
John Henderson – Fenians.

1992 – 1996
Pat Dwyer – Carrickshock United.

1997
Pat O'Neill – Gowran Young Irelands. Played in Leinster Championship.
Liam Simpson – Bennettsbridge. Played in All-Ireland quarter-final.
Eddie O'Conner – Glenmore. Played in All-Ireland semi-final.

1998
Pat O'Neill – Gowran. Young Irelands.

1999
Canice Brennan – Conahy Shamrocks.

2000 – 2005
Noel Hickey – Dunamaggin.
Sean Meally – Cloneen. Played in the 2000 Leinster semi-final.
John Tennyson – Carrickshock United. Played in 2005 All-Ireland quarter final and semi final.

2006
JJ Delaney – Fenians. Played in Leinster Championship and All-Ireland quarter final.

Noel Hickey – Dunamaggin. Played in All-Ireland semi-final and final.

2007
Noel Hickey – Dunamaggin.
John Tennyson – Carrickshock United. Played in part of Leinster semi-final.
Donncha Cody – James Stephens. Played in part of Leinster final.
Brian Hogan – O'Loughlin Gaels. Played in part of All-Ireland final.

2008
JJ Delaney – Fenians. Played in Leinster Championship.
Noel Hickey – Dunamaggin. Played in All-Ireland semi-final and final.

2009
JJ Delaney – Fenians.

2010
Noel Hickey – Dunamaggin.

2011
Noel Hickey – Dunamaggin. Played in Leinster final, All-Ireland semi-final and All-Ireland final.
JJ Delaney – Fenians. Played in Leinster semi-final.

2012
JJ Delaney – Fenians.
Noel Hickey – Dunamaggin. Played in part of Leinster semi-final, all of Leinster final and part of All-Ireland semi-final and final replay.

Also available from
IRISH SPORTS PUBLISHING

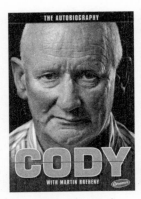

Cody: The Autobiography
Martin Breheny
ISBN 978-0-9563598-0-3

Doyle: The Greatest Hurling Story Ever Told
John Harrington
ISBN 978-0-9563598-5-8

Life Death and Hurling
Michael Duignan
ISBN 978-0-9563598-6-5

Cody is the remarkable story of the most successful GAA manager of all time. Cody has led Kilkenny hurlers to unprecedented success. Here he explains the philosophies and motivations underpinning his achievements and gives a unique insight into the life of a man whose name has become a symbol for all those who strive for success.

John Doyle hurled 19 Championship campaigns in the blue and gold of Tipperary. In that time he won eight All-Ireland senior titles and 10 Munster Senior Championships. His haul of 11 National League medals has never been equalled.
John Doyle was a one off – he was a hurling hero. This is his story.

In his autobiography, Michael Duignan lays bare the events, both personal and professional, which have gone into shaping him over the years.
A strong, true voice that speaks on sport, life and death with authority and compassion, *Life, Death & Hurling* is an exceptional work by any standards.